Richard Levin
November 7, 1974

MILTON
and
THE MILTONIC DRYDEN

MILTON
AND
THE MILTONIC DRYDEN

ANNE DAVIDSON FERRY

HARVARD UNIVERSITY PRESS
CAMBRIDGE, MASSACHUSETTS
1968

Distributed in Great Britain
by Oxford University Press, London

Library of Congress Catalog Card Number 68-25608

Printed in the United States of America

Publication of this volume has been aided by a grant
from the Hyder Edward Rollins Fund

To my parents

Acknowledgments

For the free time necessary to complete this book I am indebted to the American Association of University Women, which awarded me the Florence R. Sabin Fellowship for 1966–67. To my students at Harvard University from 1958 to 1966 I am grateful for the willingness with which they listened to many of the ideas developed here, for their suggestions, their criticisms, and their interest in this sort of exploration of literary history. The reading of *Samson Agonistes* was originally offered in lectures for Professor Reuben Brower's Humanities 6; the staff and students of that course were a continuing source of enlightenment and support. To Professor Brower I am especially thankful for advice and generous encouragement, as well as for many ideas learned from his writings, from his lectures, and from our many conversations. To Miss Marjorie Nicolson, Professor Emeritus of English Literature at Columbia University, whose lectures on *Paradise Lost* have had a shaping influence on my approach in this book, I am also grateful for many years of friendly direction. Discussions with Mary Ann Youngren, Assistant Professor of English at Wellesley College, and William Youngren, Associate Professor of English at Smith College, have continually sharpened and enriched my knowledge of later seventeenth-century literature. To my husband, David Ferry, Professor of English at Wellesley College, I can never adequately express my gratitude for his interest in the book, for the innumerable improvements which I owe to his detailed criticisms of the argument, and for all that I have learned from his ways of talking about poetry.

A. D. F.

Cambridge, Massachusetts
May 1967

Contents

MILTON
and
THE MILTONIC DRYDEN

Introduction: Literary Connections

Literary history has traditionally separated Milton and Dryden into "worlds apart."[1] We have institutionalized their separateness in courses of literature, period studies, and anthologies, which usually locate Milton in the earlier seventeenth century, while placing Dryden as the representative figure in Restoration literature. The very choice of the term "Restoration" (rather than, for example, "Post-Revolution") for the later years of the century emphasizes Dryden's identification with the age and Milton's alienation from it. This separation, then, would seem to imply a chronological division marking an historical difference in sensibility and language.

The grounds for placing the two writers in different periods of literature are only incidentally chronological, however, just as the traditional groupings of Donne's *Songs and Sonets* with Jacobean poetry, or Shakespeare's sonnets with Elizabethan, depend very little upon their dates of composition or publication.

Milton was indeed born twenty-three years before Dryden, and died when the younger poet was only forty-three, but Milton's major poems were written or completed after 1660, and his literary reputation in the later seventeenth-century was made almost entirely by their publication. Dryden, himself already an established poet, was one of the early admirers of *Paradise Lost*.[2]

The habit of assigning Milton and Dryden to different periods, then, depends less precisely on the facts of chronology than on our traditional reading of literary history. This traditional interpretation reaches back as far as attitudes toward these poets expressed in their own time, and was even perhaps encouraged by the position in English literature which each of the two writers claimed for himself.

When Dryden, the year before *Paradise Lost* was first published, represented himself as one of the speakers in *An Essay of Dramatic Poesy,* he gave himself the pseudonym of Neander, the "new man." The title was a modest and flattering way to distinguish himself from the other figures in the dialogue, aristocratic literati already "known to all the town." But to call himself the "new man" showed as much confidence as deference. The name suggests that the eyes of "all the town" will soon be upon him, that he will be singled out as a celebrated figure on the literary scene, and more interestingly it reveals Dryden's identification of himself as belonging specifically to his own generation, a "new age," a "modern" world.

This conscious, even self-conscious, identification with his own time pervades the *Essay*. It is a conversation imagined to have taken place on a specific day of the preceding year (June 3, 1665), in London, among a recognizable group of Dryden's contemporaries. Their

real identities are only perfunctorily hidden behind
Greek pseudonyms whose classical flavor suggests
merely a graceful analogy with ancient literary society
rather than the sense of identity with the past which
allowed Jonson, for example, with no incongruity, to
people the Sidneys' home in "To Penshurst" with
Dryads, Pan, Bacchus and the Muses.

Throughout the *Essay* Dryden speaks to his own
generation as distinct from their "ancient" ancestors
and from their English "forefathers" of the previous
age. The pronouns "we" and "us," whose profusion
contributes to the sociable, almost conversational tone
of the dialogue, place Dryden among his contemporaries, especially the courtly and upper-class London
theatre-going audience. His "we" and "our" sometimes refer to all Englishmen (when he alludes to
"our" war with the Dutch or makes contrasts with the
national character of the French), seldom to human
beings in general, virtually never to all Christians—
in contrast, for example, with Sidney's practice in his
Defence of Poesy, an essay perhaps even more aristocratic in tone yet still inclusive in its references to all
humanity.

Dryden's sense of himself as a "new man" of
letters, while it declares differences with poets of the
past, at the same time implies an image in his mind of
literary history as a kind of linear development from
one generation of writers to another. All the speakers
in the *Essay of Dramatic Poesy* are made to "acknowledge how much our poesy is improved by the happi-
ness of some writers yet living" or "who lately were,"
poets praised for teaching younger English writers
qualities suited for the "conversation of a gentleman"
talking to a new society with manners and tastes different from the previous age.[3] The suggestion in this

tribute, and throughout the dialogue, is of a continuous development in literature, reflecting changes in the history of the nation and in the social world to which poets address themselves. To be of the present is therefore to follow a direction in literature, and that notion implies as well a continuity with the future: Dryden seems to have sensed that his chosen modes of writing reflected the ways in which his world and therefore inevitably its poetry were changing.[4]

Milton's image of literary history was not of a line along which some point marked his position in relation to other writers belonging to different periods but, let us say, of a circle; he imagined it as a timeless society of the great, rather than a family tree. The poetic models to whom he paid tribute in both prose and poetry were not "forefathers" so much as teachers first and then associates; they were not his countrymen of previous generations nor any English writers "yet living" but ancient and Renaissance authors who, by the seventeenth century, had themselves come to be imagined almost as literary metaphors more than historical figures, immortals rather than men belonging to a specific chronological period. The image which Milton presents of himself as poet is not of a "new man" whose writings reflect the concerns of "all the town" in his own generation, but of an ancient bard with his "garland and singing robes about him" or a prophet like Isaiah whom God enriches "with all utterance and knowledge" when he "sends out his seraphim, with the hallowed fire of his altar, to touch and purify the lips."[5] The audience he addresses in poetry and prose is characteristically as inclusive as his subject and argument will allow,[6] not a special generation and class of readers, but lovers of the ancient ideals of virtue and freedom to which all poets of every period and their readers should be dedicated.

Dryden, then, presented himself as belonging especially to his own generation, speaking to it and in another way speaking for it to later writers and their readers as its representative voice. Milton identified himself as poet with literary heroes of the past whose achievement seemed to transcend history, who spoke to all men, who represented no particular age but the timeless power of poetry itself. In some sense, then, the positions in literary history which these poets claimed for themselves encourage our traditional separation of them into different periods. For the images of the ancient bard and the "new man" easily suggest a distinction in time—earlier and later generations. Dryden, in his own terms, belongs to the Restoration period as Milton never claimed for himself.

These different presentations of themselves as poets coincided with the ways in which their contemporaries placed them. When in 1668, the year after *Paradise Lost* was first published, warrant was issued to create Dryden poet laureate, his image of himself as the "new man" was officially confirmed. Although his own as yet most ambitious attempt at heroic poetry, *Annus Mirabilis,* written in the same year as the *Essay,* could not be compared even by sympathetic readers in scope or magnitude to Milton's epic, Dryden was recognized as the chief poet of the courtly world, and his literary virtues as well as his politics were identified with the interests and temper of the age. This acknowledgement of his position as leader and representative of the literary scene (demonstrated especially by his popularity as a writer of prologues and epilogues, where he dictated confidently to his contemporary audience) was articulated almost as often by attacks as by imi-

tation and praise. Both forms of recognition expressed
the sense of his timeliness, and it was precisely this
quality that Milton seemed to lack when the two poets
came to be compared: a number of the earliest printed
comments on *Paradise Lost* see it as the embodiment
of "old fashioned" qualities. Even Milton himself
showed awareness of these terms of contrast with
poetry of the "new" age when he added to the fifth
binding of the first edition of *Paradise Lost* his con-
tentious defense of blank verse as an "ancient liberty
recover'd to Heroic Poem from the troublesom and
modern bondage of Rimeing."[7] More explicitly,
Marvell, sympathetic to Milton in poetry as well as
politics, reveals (in his commendatory lines prefixed
to the second edition of *Paradise Lost* in 1674) what
seem to have been the prevailing terms of contrast
between his two greatest literary contemporaries:

> Well mightst thou scorn thy Readers to allure
> With tinkling Rhime, of thy own sense secure;
> While the *Town-Bayes* writes all the while and spells,
> And like a Pack-horse tires without his Bells:
> Their Fancies like our Bushy-points appear,
> The Poets tag them, we for fashion wear.
> I too transported by the Mode offend,
> And while I meant to Praise thee must Commend.
> Thy Verse created like thy Theme sublime,
> In Number, Weight, and Measure, needs not Rhime.[8]

Marvell, following the lead of Milton's Preface, concentrates specifically on the current preference for
couplets (represented in Dryden's rhymed adaptation
of *Paradise Lost, The State of Innocence*)[9] as the
focus of contrast between the virtues of Milton's
poetry and Dryden's fashionable appeal. Defending

Paradise Lost, he attempts to turn the distinction between "old" and "new" styles of verse into a contrast between "sublime" poetry which transcends the fashions of any time and modishness which in literature as in costume is affected and ephemeral. For all his contempt of fashion, however, the very epithet *"Town"* which Marvell attaches to the satirical pseudonym *"Bayes"* [10] acknowledges Dryden's identification with the interests of London's society of letters and his reigning position there, perhaps even more strikingly admitted by Marvell's association of the rhyming "Mode" with Dryden when in fact Marvell himself had written in rhymed couplets before Dryden had begun to learn that art.

To many admirers of Dryden, however, his contemporaneity was precisely the grounds of his superiority to Milton. They recognized and applauded his accommodation to the tastes of the new age, which they associated with the same audience he commanded in the theatre, the "we" of *An Essay of Dramatic Poesy.* Milton, by comparison, seemed to represent the "old fashioned" sensibility of a less "refined" society. A fulsome illustration of this attitude appeared in some lines from Nathaniel Lee's commendatory poem prefixed to Dryden's adaptation of *Paradise Lost,* written in 1674 but not published until 1677. Only three years after his death, Milton seemed to Lee to belong decisively to an age which had passed:

To the dead bard your fame a little owes,
For Milton did the wealthy mind disclose,
And rudely cast what you could well dispose:
He roughly drew, on an old fashioned ground,
A chaos; for no perfect world was found,
Till through the heap your mighty genius shined:

He was the golden ore, which you refined.
He first beheld the beauteous rustic maid,
And to a place of strength the prize conveyed:
You took her thence; to court this virgin brought,
Drest her with gems, new weaved her hard-spun
    thought,
And softest language, sweetest manners taught;
Till from a comet she a star doth rise,
Not to affright, but please, our wondering eyes.[11]

There is a good deal of absurdity in Lee's praise, which turns Dryden first into a godlike Creator and then into a kind of seducer (like Milton's Satan) luring to court a rustic virgin who is also somehow a blue-stocking, and pressing upon her sophisticated temptations. Yet there is in the fable a suggestion too of one possible motive for Dryden's revision of Milton's epic, an impulse to "refine" what seemed to him as to fellow writers like Lee, with whom he collaborated in the theatre, to be "old fashioned" poetry according to the "sweetest manners" of the new age.[12] This impulse is again applauded in the commendatory verses to *Absalom and Achitophel,* which acknowledge Dryden's debt to Milton with perhaps greater justice but in similar terms of contrast:

As if a Milton from the dead arose,
Filed off the rust, and the right party chose.[13]

In this view, the rust had apparently accumulated upon Milton's language as well as his political and religious affiliations. Dryden is then represented as the modern poet revising old materials according to the sympathies, and in the language, of his own generation.

If our traditional separation of Milton and Dry-

den as though they belonged in different worlds
has been encouraged by the claims of the poets themselves and by the ways in which their contemporaries
contrasted them, our interpretation of literary history
has been still more strongly influenced by the character of poetry in the succeeding period. Because Pope,
the great poet of the next generation, was able to learn
so much from Dryden, their relationship constitutes
a "line" of development which makes Dryden the
harbinger of a new style, and therefore implies that
Milton, in so far as Dryden differed from him, represented literature of an age that was past. That is to
say, critics following the example of Dr. Johnson, have
continued to stress Pope's undeniably great indebtedness to Dryden, and have therefore traced the "line"
of development in terms which confirm Dryden's
notion of his place in the continuum of English literature.[14] Reuben Brower, for example, has phrased this
conception in deliberate extremes:

After Dryden—it is tempting to say—if there had
not been a Pope, it would have been necessary to invent him. It is a commonplace of literary history that
Pope supplied the 'correct' Augustan poet required
by Dryden's most famous critical formula . . .[15]

This traditionally accepted retrospective view is supported by our recognition of the important similarities
among the works of Dryden and Pope as well as by
Pope's own sense of his poetic education. It also
coincides with Dryden's conception of himself as a
writer fully of his times whose style almost inevitably
represented the trend that was to prevail among the
next generation of poets. It is a view which has
committed us therefore to emhasizing as the essential

and distinguishing features of his work those "more obvious ways in which Dryden's practice prepared the ground for Pope's achievement . . ."

. . . his discovery of new couplet rhythms and a style appropriate for public address and manly debate, his development of a 'true heroic' narrative manner, and, more important, his creation of the allusive mode that Pope later refined and elaborated for his special purposes as moralist and satirist.[16]

This emphasis itself encourages contrasts between Dryden and Milton, since it defines Dryden's poetry (and the literary age it is said to represent) precisely by the ways in which it seems least like Milton's, by those qualities which were felt to express new interests, which led to the preference for different genres, the invention of distinctive voices in literature.

There is, then, historical support for the traditional contrast between Milton and Dryden. It has its beginnings in their own time; it is encouraged by their definitions of themselves as poets and by the later course of English poetry. What is certainly far more important to our sense òf their differences is that our most immediate responses to their writings are to those qualities by which they may be distinguished from each other. The first adjectives we might choose to describe their major works would easily define their large differences.

Yet our traditional contrast between these two poets has had its misleading influence. It has encouraged us to oversimplify our definition of the period in which their major works were written, in ways that the connections among those works deny. It has also tended to harden our responses to their poetry into fixed patterns which the writings themselves contradict.

The works of Milton and Dryden challenge our historical ordering of Restoration literature by their particular qualities and also by their relationships. Our definition of the age according to characteristics which make Dryden the "new man" pointing the way for the next literary generation has forced us to label Milton's major poems as "anachronisms," with the implication that they make no meaningful connections with other works of later seventeenth-century literature, whose authors were responsive to the nature of their own time. Yet Milton's major works—it is one intention of this book to demonstrate in detail— offered Dryden the possibility of a rich variety of suggestive connections, especially in his finest long poem, *Absalom and Achitophel,* Part I,[17] and in *All for Love,* his best play.[18] These connections are of a different order from the merely casual allusions Dryden early made to Milton's minor poems, revealing familiarity without necessary sympathy;[19] different from the recasting of *Paradise Lost* in *The State of Innocence,* for which the impulse might have been the desire to "refine" and therefore modernize "old fashioned" verse; and different too from the tributes of Dryden in verse and prose to the greatness of Milton, which testify to his admiration without demonstrating congeniality of interest.[20] The nature of the connections to be discussed in this book do not point to a development within either writer's work nor to a developing pattern of influence by Milton upon Dryden. What they do demonstrate is that the two greatest poets of the later seventeenth century at different times in their careers explored experience in significantly related styles, that Dryden in two of his most successful works was able to learn in a variety of ways from his older contemporary. The order in which these works are discussed—*Absalom and Achitophel* with *Paradise Lost, All for Love* with *Samson Agonistes*—is therefore dictated by the nature of the connections among them rather than by the chronology of either author.

In *Absalom and Achitophel* Dryden established comparisons between his satire and *Paradise Lost* as elaborate, articulated, and pointed as the relationship between any two poems in English literature; these comparisons are as richly suggestive as the connections between his works and those of Pope.[21] Dryden borrowed the large outlines of his poem and many details of design, much of his heroic manner and numberless specific expressions as well as habits of language from *Paradise Lost,* with the result that his own story may be read as a kind of re-enactment of Milton's epic, its meaning enriched by the reader's recognition of that relationship. This intricate pattern of connections, because it is woven into the very fabric of Dryden's poem, suggests that within Milton's epic he found for his own purposes more than an heroic fable and a magniloquent manner.[22] He found some fullness of meaning in Milton's language that could be assimilated into his own interpretation of experience.

All for Love, Dryden's recasting of Shakespeare's *Antony and Cleopatra,* was written four years before *Absalom and Achitophel,* in 1677. Some impulse to modernize "old fashioned" material may have inspired this work, as the same intention may have earlier moved him to revise *Paradise Lost.*[23] Certainly Dryden's own play, however numerous its verbal borrowings from the original, is profoundly alien to the mood and meaning of Shakespeare's drama. In its most peculiar qualities, its most consistently expressed view, it resembles more significantly Milton's *Samson Agonistes,* with which Dryden was familiar as early as 1675—we know from his use of it in *Aureng-Zebe*— and from which he borrowed again in *Œdipus* of 1678.[24] There are many important parallels between *All for Love* and *Samson Agonistes,* which constitute a special kind of literary relationship between the two works.[25] This relationship is altogether different from the elaborately articulated connections between *Absalom and Achitophel* and *Paradise Lost.* Dryden in *All for Love* does not have the deliberate air of setting himself to learn from Milton, as he does in the satire. He never seems to call attention to the parallels between the two works; conscious recognition of their literary relationship is not a way of developing his meaning. Yet the similarities suggest that Dryden's response to *Samson Agonistes* was none the less profoundly felt, perhaps, for being less consciously articulated. It is as if, seeking to reinterpret his hero's experience according to views less inaccessible to him than Shakespeare's, he was attracted by a more congenial dramatic form and style in the work of a contemporary. The confusions we shall see in *All for Love* imply that the direction of his revision was not predetermined, that Dryden was not fully aware of his own mixed conceptions, and that he therefore may not have recognized the ways in which his alterations of Shakespeare created parallels between his play and *Samson Agonistes.* Yet the extensive resemblances between *All for Love* and Milton's poem, in their most peculiar qualities, show Dryden's sympathy with certain meanings expressed in Milton's work. Dryden's interpretation of experience in *All for Love,* although it is not the vision presented in *Samson Agonistes,* shows so many parallel concerns, attitudes, and feelings—expressed in a style similar in so many of its most special uses—that the two dramas appear to be the work of poets not imaginatively "worlds apart" but preoccupied with very nearly the same questions.

Phrased in the largest terms, these are questions, to be sure, which concern all poets, about human experience and the power of language to interpret that experience. But the connections between the two dramas —and we shall also set the epic and the satire beside them—suggest that Milton and Dryden sought to answer these questions in ways showing profound affinities between them, despite their easily categorized differences. The richness and variety of connections among major works of Dryden and Milton indicate that they faced similar difficulties, found parallel means of resolving them, when they sought a language for poetry (that Dryden in two of his finest works could learn in large part from Milton) with which to interpret human experience as it appeared to them in the chaotic years of the later seventeenth century. These literary connections therefore complicate our definition of Restoration literature. For they deny the separation of Milton and Dryden into "worlds apart" and therefore question the identification of later seventeenth-century literature with those qualities in Dryden's verse that differ most from Milton's poetry.

The varied relationships between works of Dryden and Milton not only challenge our definition of the literary period in which they were written; they also unsettle the fixed patterns of response to their writings which our traditional contrast between them has supported. For one effect of this historical view is to encourage a monolithic conception of each writer, to make each seem to express a more consistent view of experience in a more uniform style than his works in fact reveal. We are seduced into such statements as "the Dryden of the satires is the real Dryden," as if only those qualities which readily make him a spokesman for his society or uniquely predict the accomplishments of Pope were to be interpreted as reflecting his "real" feelings and attitudes.[26] We are therefore led to ignore other qualities of his poetry which link him with Milton and which may be as distinctive and expressive, but less helpful in placing him in our traditional interpretation of literary history. We are also encouraged to overlook the very marked inconsistencies, confusions, and contradictions we shall find even within Dryden's best works, as well as the large differences between them. In similar fashion, our responses to Milton's works have been hardened by our ways of contrasting him with Dryden. We are committed to the view of Milton as a poet disillusioned, perhaps, by the later political events of his lifetime, yet continuing to cherish the same ideals, to reargue the same principles in every work, despite the fact that in his two greatest long poems, *Paradise Lost* and *Samson Agonistes,* he expresses his interpretations of experience in altogether different forms and styles.[27] The character of particular works of Milton and Dryden, and the connections between them—it is another intention of this book to demonstrate—show that neither writer can be fitted into the image of him encouraged by our traditional ways of contrasting them.

Both Dryden and Milton, themselves involved as writers in the great upheavals of the seventeenth century, felt their destructive impact on society, its values and its language, and therefore directly upon its literature. As Dryden wrote in the *Essay of Dramatic Poesy:*

. . . we have been so long together bad Englishmen, that we had not leisure to be good poets. . . . as if (in an age of so much horror) wit, and those milder studies of humanity, had no farther business among us.[28]

Although they must have disagreed about the definition of "bad Englishmen" (and at least when this was written, perhaps also of "good poets"), yet Milton and Dryden shared the sense of present need to create a language for poetry which would forge some meaningful relation between the "horror" of history as they experienced it and "those milder studies of humanity" to which poets of the past devoted themselves, or, between the events of human life, and ideal images. They showed this concern in the four major works to be discussed in this book by reshaping familiar Biblical and classical and contemporary materials in original ways as legends of the morality of language.

Of course the large assumption that language and morality are inseparable in human experience is one that Milton and Dryden inherited from earlier English, as well as classical and continental, poets and critics. Milton could look directly to Sidney or Dryden to Jonson for inspiration in the poet's dedicated search for a mode of utterance, a style that would clarify the connections between experience in the fallen world and moral ideals. They could find in Shakespeare's chronicles and Roman plays especially the most ruthless probing into the effects of political and social expediency upon the moral fabric of language. Or they could turn to classical sources—to Plato's *Gorgias,* in which Socrates ironically questions the rhetorician about the ethical implications of his verbal "art," and to Aristotle's *Rhetoric,* where he associates debased forms of rhetorical persuasion with political and moral trickery.

In the four works discussed here, when Milton and Dryden give examples of human corruption, they illustrate it as did their predecessors, by allowing characters they create to demonstrate various confusions and debasings of speech, though with a new emphasis upon verbal chaos as the separation of words from original or authoritatively sanctioned meanings. Because this emphasis can too easily be traced to the influence of "science," Hobbesian philosophy, growing scepticism or secularism or factionalism, one is tempted to isolate it as the distinguishing historical feature of Restoration writing, separating it from earlier seventeenth-century poetry. To make the distinction precisely here, however, is to ignore the fact that within their major works neither Milton nor Dryden interprets the morality of language from a consistent point of view. We can find in the writings of both these poets the most radical, the most extreme alterations in fundamental attitudes—a lack of consistency which in itself may be a distinctive feature of later seventeenth-century poetry.

Part One

PARADISE LOST
and
ABSALOM and ACHITOPHEL

I

POETIC CONTEXTS:
PARODY, IMITATION, ALLUSION

Dryden's *The State of Innocence* is an offensive
vulgarization of *Paradise Lost*. Milton's immense epic
is reduced to a scenario which in the eighteenth century
was performed as a puppet show.[1] Everything rich and
grand and strange is made coarse and mean and familiar. The vast and mysterious world of pre-history
evoked by Milton's poem is rendered in the current
clichés of Restoration drama and satire. Newly created Eve is a coquette, who by instinct feels that Adam
"long should beg, I long deny."[2] Adam's characteristic
tone before the Fall is peevish complaint, especially
against God's gift of free will: " 'Twould show more
grace my frailty to confine" [IV, i, p. 155]. Satan is a
burlesque of a rebellious politician who stirs the fallen
angels "to rise States-General of hell" [I, i, p. 129].
The often appalling contrast with *Paradise Lost* implies not only laziness and haste in Dryden's composition but absolute incomprehension of Milton and lack
of responsiveness to his language.[3] *The State of Inno-*

cence suggests that Dryden was incapable of learning anything from *Paradise Lost,* that the two poets were indeed ''worlds apart.''

Yet the familiarity with Milton's epic demanded for that exercise in revision seems actually to have taught him a great deal, to have made *Paradise Lost* somehow available for Dryden as a source of inspiration, for imitation, allusion, parody.[4] In 1678, four years after he had written *The State of Innocence,* Dryden showed in the brilliant mock-heroic style of *MacFlecknoe* that Milton's language could be assimilated to serve his poetic needs. In 1681 in *Absalom and Achitophel* he created an extraordinarily rich and complex analogy with *Paradise Lost.* That work owes its design and many of its most effective uses of language to Milton's epic. Where he failed in *The State of Innocence,* Dryden triumphed in the heroic satire. *Absalom and Achitophel* is a powerful imaginative transformation of *Paradise Lost* into a new vision which is Dryden's finest long poem.

The world of *Absalom and Achitophel* is the world of England after the Restoration, in which Dryden and Milton both lived, although the specific events comprising the action of the poem occurred seven years after the death of Milton. The upheavals surrounding the choice of successor to Charles II concerned Dryden as a royalist sympathizer and spokesman. They were religious and political disturbances such as those to which Milton had devoted twenty years of polemical writing, although in his poems he never alluded in detail to the present scene, very rarely acknowledged his attitudes to be those of a specific party or his accents to belong to a distinctive social class. When Dryden chose the royal succession and the Popish Plot for his poetic materials, however, he wished no more than

Milton to limit his interest to the merely local and fac-
tional. As a propagandist he aimed to persuade his
audience that large issues of timeless and universal
significance were at stake, and as a poet (especially one
with ambitions to contribute in the heroic mode) he
must have intended to interest more readers than the
contemporaries with whom he habitually identified
himself, the "we" of the earlier *Essay of Dramatic
Poesy*.

Like Milton, Dryden claims authority and univer-
sality for his poem by telling, or pretending to tell, a
Biblical story, and, like the narrator in *Paradise Lost*
—who traces the origins of "all our woe" [I, 3]—Dryden's speaker explicitly addresses himself to an audience of all fallen humanity:

> But, when to Sin our byast Nature leans,
> The carefull Devil is still at hand with means;
> And providently Pimps for ill desires . . .
>
> [79-81]

This interpretive comment, coming after the traditional epic summary of past events, introduces the
present action of the poem with the suggestion that
Absalom and Achitophel be read in a particular relation to the story of the Fall, which for readers of English poetry had so recently been incorporated into the
epic tradition in *Paradise Lost*. The interpretation is
phrased in general terms characteristic of such
"author-comments" in epic poetry: "Sin," "our byast Nature," "ill desires." The indefinite "when" and
the continuous present tense lift the moral occasion
out of any specific place and time; the word "still"
suggests both "always" and "at any moment since the
first temptation so long ago." This generalization in-

cludes in its reference every temptation to every sin;
its sentiment could be stated (even in the same diction,
but for the deliberately jarring word "Pimps") by the
poet who narrates *Paradise Lost*. Following these
three lines is the announcement of the satire's occasion. This is a particular instance or effect of a general
law. What has been said of "our byast Nature" and of
the Devil's attentiveness is demonstrated by recent
English history: "The Good old Cause reviv'd, a Plot
requires" [82]. Not only do the words "Cause" and
"Plot" have more specific referents than "Sin" or
"ill desires"; the tense here refers to past action bearing fruit in the actual present, not the timeless or Latin
historical present; the narrator speaks as a man much
closer to the scene, with his slangy reference to the
"Good old Cause" which would sound quite out of
place among the epic generalizations and Biblical references of the previous three lines. The introduction
of the Plot is then followed by two lines in which the
poet, speaking from his experience of the world, places
the particular events of the poem in the endlessly recurring patterns of history:

> Plots, true or false, are necessary things,
> To raise up Common-wealths, and ruin Kings.
>
> [83-84]

By thus introducing the occasion of his satire, the eruption of the conspiracy, as a particular illustration or
result of human weakness opportunely exploited by
the Devil, Dryden allows a unique literary relationship
between his poem and *Paradise Lost*. *Absalom and
Achitophel* can be read as a particular, local, contemporary instance of the universal and timelessly recurring drama of Milton's epic.

As a modern instance of temptation and fall, *Absalom and Achitophel* follows the large outlines of *Paradise Lost*. It professes as the scene for its action an earlier world revealed to the poet in Scripture—the "pious times" of David's reign—a world to which we are in the opening lines directed to attach pastoral associations of simple spontaneity expressing what "Nature prompted" before civilization "deny'd." The hero of this later Eden is a later Adam (a comparison made explicit in Dryden's apology "To the Reader"), whom the narrator portrays in language echoing Milton's descriptions of newly created man:[5]

> In him alone, 'twas Natural to please.
> His motions all accompanied with grace;
> And *Paradise* was open'd in his face.   [28-30]

The action of the satire is the violation of that paradisal nature by a later agent of the Devil, whose successful temptation is ultimately thwarted by heavenly consent. The poem ends, like *Paradise Lost,* with the poet's vision of history "Restor'd" according to the divine plan:

> Henceforth a Series of new time began,
> The mighty Years in long Procession ran:
> Once more the Godlike *David* was Restor'd,
> And willing Nations knew their Lawfull Lord.
>   [1028-1031]

The parallels between *Absalom and Achitophel* and Milton's story direct our reading of Dryden's poem; using allusion, imitation, parody, he invites us to compare his presentation of current history with *Paradise Lost.*

That comparison includes within it the greatest possible variety of other literary connections. It offers the story of Adam and Eve as the archetypal model for all human history, so that the resemblances of the satire to *Paradise Lost* enable Dryden to include within that larger analogy further parallels with other literary renderings of the primary patterns of experience. For example, as passages later discussed will show, the similarity between Achitophel's tempting of Absalom and Satan's of Adam and Eve, includes further literary parallels with Shakespearean scenes of political temptation—especially Henry IV's cynical advice to Prince Hal[6]—and with the formulas for sexual seduction traditional to lyric poetry. The large parallels with *Paradise Lost* gather the richness of literary allusions in *Absalom and Achitophel* into an organic whole in still another fashion. Milton's epic language, later analyses will emphasize, is itself an elaborately woven fabric of literary adaptations. Dryden's ways of suggesting that his satire be read in comparison with *Paradise Lost* therefore involve further connections with Biblical literature, with heroic and pastoral poetry, and with other traditions assimilated into Milton's own style. By establishing this comparison, Dryden creates an inclusive literary and moral context for his contemporary political materials.

The form of Miltonic borrowing for which Dryden's earlier works prepare us is ironic parody. Both the clumsy vulgarizing in *The State of Innocence* and the highly controlled debasing of epic style in *Mac-Flecknoe*—especially the vision of the monarch of dull poets like Satan "High on a Throne of his own Labours rear'd" [107][7]—predict the use of *Paradise Lost* for absurd comparisons. We are not surprised to find Dryden in *Absalom and Achitophel* exploiting for his satirical purposes the vast disparity in scale and significance, already suggested in the notion of the Devil as a pimp, between the petty vulgarities of modern life and the grandeur of Milton's heroic world.

The most elaborate example of ironic parody is Dryden's series of portraits of the enemy party, which by its adaptation of details borrowed from *Paradise Lost,* draws a contrast between Milton's epic catalogue of fallen angels and the satirist's roll-call of cheats, ignoramuses, hypocrites, debauchees. While Milton's catalogue, as part of an extended comparison of devils to traditional epic warriors, lends grandeur and glamor to the fallen angels, Dryden's comparison of the King's enemies to Miltonic devils measures the loss of heroic stature even in modern wickedness.

The narrator of *Paradise Lost* introduces his catalogue of Satan's host:

Forthwith from every Squadron and each Band
The Heads and Leaders thither hast where stood
Their great Commander; Godlike shapes and forms
Excelling human, Princely Dignities,
And Powers that earst in Heaven sat on Thrones;
Though of their Names in heav'nly Records now
Be no memorial, blotted out and ras'd
By thir Rebellion, from the Books of Life.
Nor had they yet among the Sons of *Eve*
Got them new Names, till wandring ore the Earth,
Through Gods high sufferance for the tryal of man,
By falsities and lyes the greatest part
Of Mankind they corrupted to forsake
God their Creator, and th' invisible
Glory of him, that made them, to transform

Oft to the Image of a Brute, adorn'd
With gay Religions full of Pomp and Gold,
And Devils to adore for Deities:
Then were they known to men by various Names,
And various Idols through the Heathen World.
[I, 356-375]

This elevated epic language is very different from
the comparable passage in *Absalom and Achitophel*:

Titles and Names 'twere tedious to Reherse
Of Lords, below the Dignity of Verse.
Wits, warriors, Common-wealthsmen, were the best:
Kind Husbands and meer Nobles all the rest.
And, therefore in the name of Dulness, be
The well hung *Balaam* and cold *Caleb* free.
And Canting *Nadab* let Oblivion damn,
Who made new porridge for the Paschal Lamb.
Let Friendships holy band some Names assure:
Some their own Worth, and some let Scorn secure.
[569-578]

Dryden's catalogue is not, like Milton's, a serious imitation of the epic convention, for although the narrator
sometimes speaks almost in the voice of an heroic poet
—"Let Friendships holy band some Names assure"—
the epic manner here is totally ironic. It is used for
assertions the opposite of those that an heroic poet
would make: "their own Worth" will secure these
names not fame and honor, but oblivion. And it is
debased by other uses of language incompatible with
an epic manner.

The force of this parodic style depends on more
than the implied likening of the enemy faction to devils.
The speaker's satiric vision of his opponents sharpens

as the language builds a comparison with the epic catalogue from *Paradise Lost* by the adaptation of various
kinds of details borrowed from the original. For example, Milton's resonant list of "Godlike shapes and
forms / Excelling human, Princely Dignities" suggests
comparison with Dryden's far less glamorous series of
"Wits, warriors, Common-wealthsmen" who are defined according to categories which place people in
society by their occupation and their party allegiance
rather than, as Milton's angels are placed, by their
position in the hierarchy of God's creation. Even more
emphatically Dryden transforms Milton's "Powers
that earst in Heaven sat on Thrones." In the sequence
of the satirical passage their counterparts are "Kind
Husbands and meer Nobles," distinguished only by
their social titles and their mild domestic virtues, or
even perhaps by their sexual prowess, which the nature
of many personal references in the rest of the passage
suggests may be one meaning for "Kind Husbands."
More precisely Dryden echoes the lines in which
Milton's narrator declares his catalogue to be a list
of forgotten titles:

Though of their Names in heav'nly Records now
Be no memorial, blotted out and ras'd
By thir Rebellion, from the Books of Life.

[361-363]

The imperative construction and the alliteration of
b sounds give firmness and severity to the epic poet's
judgment: it has theological finality, which Dryden's
narrator turns into quite another sort of judgment.
By phrases like "in the name of Dulness" and "let
Oblivion damn" he suggests a kind of social boredom
echoing the polite *ennui* of "tedious" in the first line.

These expressions were probably also read by Dryden's contemporaries as part of a theatrical metaphor: Nadab is a tiresome playwright whose performance is "damned" by the critic "Oblivion."[8] This social and aesthetic dismissal is supported by the nature of the personal references to contemporary figures: Balaam, Caleb, and Nadab apparently represent men well known for their sexual behavior. Caleb, for example, whose epic epithet is "cold," was identified (in the Key to the allegory published with the poem in 1716) as Lord Grey of Wark, notorious for supposedly having consented to an affair between his wife and Monmouth.[9] This sort of allusion suggests, then, still another kind of judgment by the speaker; these figures are to be dismissed because they are boring and perhaps also because they are sexually improper. Both judgments are social rather than theological: they make us think of these figures not as damned souls but as unacceptable personalities. Dryden next adopts still another idea from Milton, whose fallen angels turned pagan gods set up new idols in the "Image of a Brute, adorn'd / With gay Religions full of Pomp and Gold." Such an acknowledgment of the glamor and opulence of pagan ritual is quite absent from Dryden's version:

> And Canting *Nadab* let Oblivion damn,
> Who made new porridge for the Paschal Lamb.
> [575-576]

The lines are thought to refer to William, Lord Howard of Escrick, who asserted his innocence of a libel on the court party by taking Holy Communion, swallowed in a concoction called "lamb's wool" (ale poured on roasted apples and sugar).[10] This arresting contemporary reference measures the distance between the gilded pomp of false religions as Milton conceived them and the absurdity of modern blasphemy. The phrase "new porridge for the Paschal Lamb" is a brutally coarsened and mean domestic contrast to Milton's lines concerning pagan idols: there is no glamor or opulence in porridge. The satirical point of Dryden's lines depends upon such implied contrasts, so that a full appreciation of it demands the reader's recognition of the connections between the two epic catalogues.

One more quotation from this section of the satire will illustrate the rich compression and fine precision in Dryden's parodic uses of Milton's epic style. In line 598, the phrase "The Sons of *Belial*" alludes to another passage in the Miltonic catalogue:

> *Belial* came last, then whom a Spirit more lewd
> Fell not from Heaven, or more gross to love
> Vice for it self: To him no Temple stood
> Or Altar smoak'd; yet who more oft then hee
> In Temples and at Altars, when the Priest
> Turns Atheist, as did *Ely*'s Sons, who fill'd
> With lust and violence the house of God.
> In Courts and Palaces he also Reigns
> And in luxurious Cities, where the noyse
> Of riot ascends above thir loftiest Towrs,
> And injury and outrage: And when Night
> Darkens the Streets, then wander forth the Sons
> Of *Belial*, flown with insolence and wine.
>
> [I, 490-502]

The last six lines sound almost as if they might have been intended by Milton as a reference to the riotous debauches notorious among Restoration courtiers,[11] but even there the language gives ominous grandeur to this sort of vice, a grandeur quite absent from Dryden's brilliant compression: "The Sons of *Belial* had a glorious Time." The breezy upperclass slanginess of the phrase strips the word "glorious" of its original theological and heroic connotations. In Dryden's local, modern version of Milton's archetypal world, lust and violence have no theological or heroic significance. They are merely tedious, tawdry, absurd, offenses to the poet's taste and sense of propriety rather than "injury and outrage" to the moral order of the universe.

As a form of literary adaptation, Dryden's ironic parodies do not intend disparagement of Milton's poem. Far from mocking or debasing the values expressed by the Biblical and heroic language of *Paradise Lost,* Dryden's parodic transformation of that language honors the original epic as the repository of noble ideals. Those ideals are not criticized but are themselves a criticism of the world of Dryden's satire, in which heroic and Christian values have become *only* ideals, not practised modes of behavior, not living facts of experience. Dryden's ironic parodies therefore pay tribute to Christian epic but at the same time they place the "modern" poet at a greater distance from the Biblical-heroic tradition than Milton placed the bard of *Paradise Lost.* The narrator in the satire is heir to the heroic values of Milton's epic (and of all its models), and so can speak as an heroic poet, but this is only one literary role in which he introduces himself. He does not, like Milton's narrator, identify the whole of his experience with Christian and classical literature and history, does not present himself exclusively in Biblical and traditionally poetic images. Dryden's language in the ironic parodies of Miltonic epic also identifies his narrator as a satirist living in the debased world of Restoration England, an observer of its viciousness and absurdity but also a committed spokesman for a political party and a social class, who can combine the heroic manner with other literary roles. Epic poetry, even when it is honored as the repository of noble ideals, offers one among other ways of evaluating experience: the "modern" poet can therefore parody even his most cherished models.

If *Absalom and Achitophel* is read as a contemporary and local instance of Milton's archetypal story, then Dryden's language can at once measure the distance between Milton's heroic world and the petty occurrences of history by ironic parody, and it can also evoke the memory of original grandeur by other forms of Miltonic adaptation. Ironic parody as a distinct style is indeed virtually limited in the poem to the satiric descriptions of the enemy faction or the vulgar "herd." Praising his own party in another catalogue weighty with Virgilian allusions,[12] Dryden imitates a serious heroic style, borrowing perhaps from the epic invocations of *Paradise Lost* the combined metaphor for his poem as a song and as the flight of a winged creature circling heaven and earth:

Here stop my Muse, here cease thy painfull flight;
No Pinions can pursue Immortal height:
Tell good *Barzillai* thou canst sing no more,
And tell thy Soul she should have fled before;
Or fled she with his life, and left this Verse
To hang on her departed Patron's Herse?
Now take thy steepy flight from heaven, and see
If thou canst find on earth another *He* . . .

[854-861]

The serious heroic style of this catalogue, in contrast to the ironic roll-call earlier in the poem, again draws parallels with *Paradise Lost*. The speaker uses that manner to praise the few men remaining in his world in whom heroic values are embodied, as Milton's narrator uses it to judge the false heroism of the fallen angels. By a more specific reference, Dryden then identifies the heroes honored in this serious catalogue with Milton's heavenly host, sorrowing over Satan's war against divine rule yet secure in facing a battery of infernal cannons:

> With grief they view'd such powerful Engines bent,
> To batter down the lawful Government.
>
> [917-918]

Then in the concluding section of the satire, to be discussed in detail in Chapter IV, he uses as a means of asserting the final restoration of order a serious epic manner, combining Biblical and Miltonic with classical allusions, to endow King David with authority like that of the Godhead in *Paradise Lost* [936-938, 1026-1027].

Even when he is not claiming greatness for his own party, Dryden throughout the satire follows Milton in using such traditional epic devices as extended similes and especially explicit "author-comments" upon the general moral significance of actions, which in their largeness and gravity sustain his narrator's identification with poets of the heroic tradition.

Still more common than either ironic parody or serious imitation of Milton's heroic style is another form of adaptation which can be called extended allusive comparison. This device Dryden may have learned from *Paradise Lost* itself, where Milton's presentation of Satan and his followers depends upon an extended comparison with the heroes of the epic tradition. In

Absalom and Achitophel Dryden draws a comparable extended comparison between Achitophel and Milton's Satan, with effects that parallel those created by Milton. For if we find Satan in the first two books of *Paradise Lost* to be powerful and magnificent in his wickedness, we do so largely because the poet presents him as a hellish version of the self-assertive, defiant, unyielding classical hero. While if we find Achitophel or Shaftesbury to be powerfully dangerous in his resolve "to Ruine or to Rule" and sinister in his "Implacable" hate, we do so chiefly because Dryden presents him as a contemporary Satan. The Old Testament figure of Achitophel provides virtually nothing in the portrait but his name and position.[13] Our attention is directed rather to the Miltonic comparison, and to the other literary parallels which that analogy includes. Shaftesbury, like Satan, is first in importance among the fallen host, and first to command the poet's powers of portraiture:

> Of these the false *Achitophel* was first:
> A Name to all succeeding Ages Curst.
> For close Designs, and crooked Counsels fit;
> Sagacious, Bold, and Turbulent of wit:
> Restless, unfixt in Principles and Place;
> In Power unpleas'd, impatient of Disgrace.
> A fiery Soul, which working out its way,
> Fretted the Pigmy Body to decay:
> And o'r inform'd the Tenement of Clay.
> A daring Pilot in extremity;
> Pleas'd with the Danger, when the Waves went high
> He sought the Storms; but for a Calm unfit,
> Would Steer too nigh the Sands, to boast his Wit.
> Great Wits are sure to Madness near ally'd;
> And thin Partitions do their Bounds divide:

Else, why should he, with Wealth and Honour blest,
Refuse his Age the needful hours of Rest?
Punish a Body which he coud not please;
Bankrupt of Life, yet Prodigal of Ease?
And all to leave, what with his Toyl he won,
To that unfeather'd, two Leg'd thing, a Son:
Got, while his Soul did hudled Notions try;
And born a shapeless Lump, like Anarchy.
In Friendship False, Implacable in Hate:
Resolv'd to Ruine or to Rule the State.
To Compass this the Triple Bond he broke;
The Pillars of the publick Safety shook:
And fitted *Israel* for a Foreign Yoke.
Then, seiz'd with Fear, yet still affecting Fame,
Usurp'd a Patriott's All-attoning Name.

[150-179]

There is no single passage in *Paradise Lost* to which
these lines invite extended comparison (and here as
everywhere in the poem there are many allusions to
writers other than Milton)[14] but the likeness of Achitophel-Shaftesbury to Milton's Satan is obviously intended and repeatedly called to the reader's attention
by a variety of devices. Indeed, the name "Satan"
might appropriately be substituted in our minds for
the reference to Achitophel in the first line, for Satan
is supreme above every "Name to all succeeding Ages
Curst," a claim whose sweeping inclusiveness is itself
Miltonic.[15] In the remainder of the passage there are
very few particular references to historical details of
Achitophel's or Shaftesbury's experience, and among
those references only the mention of the political
events in the last five lines is such that they could not
also apply to Milton's Satan. Elsewhere we are given,
for example, as a description of Achitophel:

> A fiery Soul, which working out its way,
> Fretted the Pigmy Body to decay . . .

These famous lines refer in part to Shaftesbury's actual physical shortness,[16] a sense in which the description could in no way apply to Milton's gigantic Satan (although his followers entering *Pandæmonium* are likened to "that Pigmean Race," I, 780); but Dryden's diction directs attention away from the literal meaning of this description to its metaphorical sense. By avoiding the personal pronoun "his," Dryden makes "*the* Pigmy Body" a metaphor for physical limits which "*A* fiery Soul" disdains: "the Pigmy Body" stands for any body, considered as opposed to, or inadequate for, any soul "fiery" with ambition like Satan, within whom a "hot Hell" burns [IX, 467]. Such transformation of particular historical references to elaborate the comparison with Satan is also illustrated by the lines attacking Shaftesbury's son:

> And all to leave, what with his Toyl he won,
> To that unfeather'd, two Leg'd thing, a Son:
> Got, while his Soul did hudled Notions try;
> And born a shapeless Lump, like Anarchy.

Again Dryden makes the language applicable to Satan as well as to Shaftesbury. His "Son" is identified by the traditional Platonic definition—"that unfeather'd, two Leg'd thing"—as Man. He is also identified as Death, for the phrase "born a shapeless Lump" alludes to Milton's first description of the figure of Death in Book II: "The other shape, / If shape it might be call'd that shape had none" [II, 666-667]. This echo of Milton's allegory (itself an imitation of Spenser's style)[17] creates further parallels between Satan and the figure in Dryden's portrait. Satan is the father of Death, born of his union with Sin, the shape who sprang from his head as the embodiment of his anarchical ambition. The progenitor of Sin and Death, Satan is also the parent of fallen man, as Dryden's combined allusions suggest, and it is to this monstrous offspring that Satan must leave the fruit of his ambition, our mortal world. Lines which are in one sense an historical reference to Shaftesbury's biography are therefore at the same time a multiple comparison with Milton's Satan, as well as a metaphor for the ashiness of ambition's fruits, and their destructiveness. Achitophel's toil, like Satan's, leaves a dangerous legacy for the whole world.

While the few specific references to historical fact in this portrait are as far as possible expressed in terms equally applicable to Satan and to Achitophel-Shaftesbury, often alluding precisely to language in *Paradise Lost,* the rest of the portrait supports the comparison by its deliberate generality, so that although we read the passage as the description of an individual, we recognize him as a representative of a type: the Satanic hero.[18] We are made to understand Achitophel by being told what variety of man he is, what category of moral being he exemplifies. In the third line of the portrait, for example, he is described "For close Designs, and crooked Counsels fit." "Close Designs" and "crooked Counsels" define a *kind* of intellectual activity. The reader does not need to know the nature of the particular designs or to whom the counsels are given in order to understand the quality of mind capable of engaging in this sort of activity. Nor does his understanding depend on hearing the precise echo of Satan urging his followers "To work in close design, by fraud or guile" [I, 646]. Dryden's diction defines a recognizable type of intellect, of which Milton's Satan with his serpentine wiles that "made intricate seem strait" [IX, 632] is the original.

This use of diction, frequently allusive, to place Achitophel in a category which includes Satan as fully as it includes the historical figure of Shaftesbury, is supported by the narrator's habit (itself reminiscent of Milton's didactic "author-comments" in *Paradise Lost*) of offering generalizations as explanations for Achitophel's particular behaviour:

> Great Wits are sure to Madness near ally'd;
> And thin Partitions do their Bounds divide . . .

Illustrative metaphor is a further means of defining the "character": "A daring Pilot in extremity." Again Achitophel is placed in a category, as a kind of person who acts in a predictable way when involved in a certain variety of experience. The category includes Satan, whose actions Milton's epic narrator compares in the scene of Eve's temptation specifically to a pilot:

> As when a Ship by skilful Stearsman wrought
> Nigh Rivers mouth or Foreland, where the Wind
> Veres oft, as oft so steers, and shifts her Saile;
> So varied hee, and of his tortuous Traine
> Curld many a wanton wreath in sight of *Eve* . . .
> [IX, 513-517]

This form of extended allusive comparison to *Paradise Lost,* unlike Dryden's ironic parodies, has a magnifying power comparable to the effects of Milton's own heroic comparisons. The pigmy politician is made to seem, like Satan, larger than life size, powerfully

dangerous, involved in actions which threaten ''all succeeding Ages.'' His temptation of Absalom, then, becomes an event of heroic proportions and universal
significance. The issues which are involved reach to
the roots of morality, for the appeals of Achitophel are
those of Satan:

> Believe me, Royal Youth, thy Fruit must be,
> Or gather'd Ripe, or rot upon the Tree.
> [250-251]

The response of Absalom is that of Adam and Eve—
''I find, I find my mounting Spirits Bold'' [367][19]—
and of all human beings who from them have inherited
''our byast Nature.'' In passages like the portrait of
Achitophel, Dryden's use of allusive comparison insists
on the significance for all men of the issues of history,
however local and ephemeral its occasions may seem
to be. The parallels with Milton's presentation of the
temptation and Fall of man imply that the tangled
circumstances of this world, no matter how petty and
passing, demand to be interpreted in moral terms because they involve moral issues. Allusive comparisons
to *Paradise Lost* are therefore used as a means of
insisting on the need to understand the recurring patterns of history in the light of enduring values, which
are most faithfully preserved by literary tradition.
This form of adaptation, differing in its chief function
from ironic parody, allows the satirist to use his literary heritage as a means of expanding his interpretation
of experience as a whole. It is because he has been educated by literature that the narrator in *Absalom and
Achitophel* can respond with conviction to the profound
moral issues that history, in its particular instances of
Milton's timeless and universal story, presents.

II

SATANIC RHETORIC

Dryden's adaptations of Miltonic language in ironic parodies, serious imitations, and allusive comparisons, by calling the reader's attention to parallels between the satire and *Paradise Lost,* create a context in which *Absalom and Achitophel* may be richly understood. Because this context is literary, because the devices of which it consists are imitations or echoes of style, they call attention to the poet's own uses of language: we are asked to respond not only to what he says, but with fine discriminations to his manner of saying it. Because the varieties of Miltonic imitation are so distinct from one another, and so often contained within such "set-pieces" as the catalogues and portraits, with their clearly marked outlines, they point to Dryden's creation of a varied poetic language. In doing so they not only recall the conscious artistry of *Paradise Lost,* with its own rich pattern of allusion and parody, but they parallel in function the numerous references by Milton's narrator to his "adventrous," "unattempted," "answerable," "unpremeditated" style.[1] Dryden, as strongly as Milton, wishes to make the reader aware of his poetic manner because, like Milton, he interprets the moral issues of his story explicitly and consistently in the light of his attitudes toward language, his views of its origin and its powers. In *Absalom and Achitophel*, as in *Paradise Lost*, both the cause and the evidence of the Fall are represented as the abuse of words. In the satire and in the epic, sin and restoration are wrought by the powers of language. Uses of words, modes of speech, styles in each poem are therefore not only instruments for the poet's expression, but central to his very subject and its meaning. This parallel concern with language as a moral force implies some more closely shared view of experience than is indicated by Dryden's ironic parodies, serious stylistic imitations, or extended allusive comparisons to Milton's work. This manner of interpreting the Fall suggests some larger reasons why Dryden was able to assimilate to his own satiric purposes many uses of language characteristic of Milton's Biblical epic style.

In *Paradise Lost* the dangers that may be wrought by language are revealed chiefly through Milton's presentation of Satan; one reason the action of the poem opens in Hell is to build from the beginning a contrast between Satan's corrupt rhetoric and the poet's inspired eloquence.[2] Repeatedly the narrator interprets Satan's speeches with reminders that his language is specious, lest the reader relax his attentiveness and so fail to distinguish the falsity of Satan's words. One of the clearest examples of this sort of guidance by the narrator follows the epic catalogue,

when Satan's oratory infuses martial virtue into the
fallen host:

> . . . but he his wonted pride
> Soon recollecting, with high words, that bore
> Semblance of worth not substance, gently rais'd
> Their fainted courage, and dispel'd their fears.
> > [I, 527-530]

Similar, less explicit warnings are frequently given,
which we learn to recognize in retrospect if not at first
reading. For instance, the narrator remarks of Satan's
first speech:

> So spake th' Apostate Angel, though in pain,
> Vaunting aloud, but rackt with deep despare . . .
> > [I, 125-126]

Especially the word ''Vaunting'' cautions us to hear
the hollowness in the heroic language of Hell. It is by
such comments that our attention is most obviously
directed to Satan's manner of speech. We are asked to
concern ourselves with his *ways* of using words, as well
as their meanings, both expressing the nature of the
evil he embodies.

The falsity distinguished by the narrator in Satan's language is demonstrated in his speeches in a
variety of ways, for Satan is a conscious master of
the arts of language and can alter his style to suit his
purposes. Within that variety there is a fatal sameness,
though, for unlike the other characters in the poem—
who praise, question, instruct, lament, confess, forgive
—Satan uses language almost exclusively to *persuade,*
and therefore the meanings of his words originate in

his will. To understand what he says the reader must refer, not to divinely sanctioned definitions such as are given, as we shall see, to the language of unfallen men and angels, but to Satan's purposes. His language is always subservient to need, and so it is willfully arbitrary, without reference to any truths outside his own mind. It has therefore a functional flexibility and an inner consistency which compose its dangerous power.

Most obviously, and from the very beginning of the poem, we see Satan manipulating language as a means of managing his armies. His first address to them is a clear example of style shaped as an instrument to bring about an end:

> Princes, Potentates,
> Warriers, the Flowr of Heav'n, once yours, now lost,
> If such astonishment as this can sieze
> Eternal spirits; or have ye chos'n this place
> After the toyl of Battel to repose
> Your wearied vertue, for the ease you find
> To slumber here, as in the Vales of Heav'n?
> Or in this abject posture have ye sworn
> To adore the Conquerour? who now beholds
> Cherube and Seraph rowling in the Flood
> With scatter'd Arms and Ensigns, till anon
> His swift pursuers from Heav'n Gates discern
> Th' advantage, and descending tread us down
> Thus drooping, or with linked Thunderbolts
> Transfix us to the bottom of this Gulfe.
> Awake, arise, or be for ever fall'n.   [I, 315-330]

Virtually every persuasive speech to his followers begins with such a resounding list of titles: "O Myriads of immortal Spirits, O Powers / Matchless, but with th' Almighty" [I, 622-623]; "Powers and Dominions, Deities of Heav'n'' [II, 11]; "O Progeny of Heav'n, Empyreal Thrones'' [II, 430]. Even his last speech, which is to be met only with "A dismal universal hiss'' of devils turned snakes, opens as if addressed to angels still in their heavenly places:

> Thrones, Dominations, Princedoms, Vertues,
>   Powers,
> For in possession such, not onely of right,
> I call ye and declare ye now . . .   [X, 460-462]

The function of this device for Satan's purpose is obvious. The very sounds of the names evoke the past glory of the angels; the appeal to their pride is stirring, and Satan's refusal to give up their titles is an assertion of his unconquerable will. In such speeches he appears glamorous and impressive as he exploits the gifts of great leaders, of military commanders, and of political orators. But his characteristic use of these flattering titles is more than a demonstration of effective public rhetoric: it is a revelation of the corruption which is at the center of Satan's consciousness and therefore inescapably expressed in all his uses of language.

The meaning of Satan's dependence on false titles is revealed in an exchange of speeches between him and Abdiel during the War in Heaven, when the virtuous angel challenges the principles supporting Satan's modes of language.[3] The first of these speeches opens with the formula associated since the opening scene with Satan's corrupt use of words:

> Thrones, Dominations, Princedomes, Vertues,
>   Powers,
> If these magnific Titles yet remain

> Not meerly titular, since by Decree
> Another now hath to himself ingross't
> All Power, and us eclipst under the name
> Of King anointed . . .   [V, 772-777]

To Satan the "magnific Titles" are descriptive, but
only of power; they become "meerly titular" when
God by arbitrary decree robs them of significance,
assuming for Himself a "name" that claims for Him
superior force. The refusal to give up what Satan sees
as the autonomous power described by these titles
is the governing argument in his revolt:

> Who can in reason then or right assume
> Monarchie over such as live by right
> His equals, if in power and splendor less,
> In freedome equal? or can introduce
> Law and Edict on us, who without law
> Erre not, much less for this to be our Lord,
> And look for adoration to th' abuse
> Of those Imperial Titles which assert
> Our being ordain'd to govern, not to serve?
>   [V, 794-802]

It is Abdiel's function to point out that this faulty
logic expresses a willful misunderstanding of the nature of language, whose divine origin is in the creative
Word of God:

> O argument blasphemous, false and proud!
> Words which no eare ever to hear in Heav'n
> Expected . . .
> . . . .
> Shalt thou give Law to God, shalt thou dispute
> With him the points of libertie, who made

Thee what thou art, & formd the Pow'rs of Heav'n
Such as he pleasd, and circumscrib'd thir being?
Yet by experience taught we know how good,
And of our good, and of our dignitie
How provident he is, how farr from thought
To make us less, bent rather to exalt
Our happie state under one Head more neer
United. But to grant it thee unjust,
That equal over equals Monarch Reigne:
Thy self though great & glorious dost thou count,
Or all Angelic Nature joind in one,
Equal to him begotten Son, by whom
As by his Word the mighty Father made
All things, ev'n thee, and all the Spirits of Heav'n
By him created in thir bright degrees,
Crownd them with Glory, & to thir Glory nam'd
Thrones, Dominatiods, Princedoms, Vertues,
    Powers
Essential Powers . . .   [V, 809-811, 822-841]

Abdiel's reply articulates the theory of language by
which the corruption of Satan's rhetoric is measured
from the beginning of the poem. It is the theory to
which Milton gives support by attributing it also to
God and Raphael, and by demonstrating its truth in
the experience of his unfallen man. According to Abdiel's argument, the titles which "nam'd" the angelic
orders originate in the same divine act that "created"
the angels "in thir bright degrees." They have heavenly authority as definitions of the beings whose nature
and place in the order of creation they were made to
designate. They do not "assert" autonomous power,
as Satan insists; they glorify, like all language, which
is itself a creation of God and therefore defines the
"Essential" nature of all creatures. Adam's first

moments as he describes them to Raphael are designed
to demonstrate the truth of this theory:

> ... to speak I tri'd, and forthwith spake,
> My Tongue obey'd and readily could name
> What e're I saw.   [VIII, 271-273]

The orderliness and ease of this first human utterance
tell us about man's created nature and also about the
origin of the words he uses. They pre-exist—as God
implies when he praises Adam for "rightly" naming
His Works [VIII, 439]—in the mind of their Creator.
Man's reason apprehends them because they and he
were created to glorify the same Maker. The names of
the "fair Creatures" that Adam "readily" discovers
naturally compose a psalm or hymn [VIII, 273-282]
to the "Author of this Universe," whose Name alone
Adam cannot utter:

> ... for thou above all these,
> Above mankinde, or aught then mankinde higher,
> Surpassest farr my naming ...   [VIII, 357-359]

Satan's rejection of this theory of language is the
measure of his corruption because it is the denial of
his creatureliness and of God's creativity. His own
debased theory is blasphemous, as Abdiel argues, because by refusing to recognize the divine origin of language he denies the creative act of the Word that
"made / All things."[4] Satan severs words as well as
the creatures they define from their necessary places
in the order of the universe, and therefore dissociates
them from their moral and theological meanings, a
profanation for which he is explicitly condemned both
by Abdiel [VI, 174-175] and earlier by Gabriel [IV,

949-951]. Words and their referents to him have become neutral, except as they may be used, the way he uses the angelic titles, to "assert" his own power.

Satan's characteristic rhetorical devices for asserting this force are flattery and sarcasm. These modes are habitually mingled in his addresses, as in the first speech to his armies, in which the rehearsal of angelic titles is followed by a series of insulting questions:

> . . . or have ye chos'n this place
> After the toyl of Battel to repose
> Your wearied vertue, for the ease you find
> To slumber here, as in the Vales of Heav'n?
> Or in this abject posture have ye sworn
> To adore the Conquerour? . . .   [I, 318-323]

This sarcastic language, like his flattering use of titles, identifies Satan as an effective orator, who exploits the traditional tools of public persuasion (such as Milton himself used in his polemical writing).[5] As evidence of the theory of language attacked by Abdiel, however, these modes are made to express the corruption of Satan's nature. For the effectiveness of his sarcasm also depends on the arbitrary choice of words imposed according to his will. His questions in this first speech are not really questions, but insults intended to move his armies. These insults depend upon the discrepancies between the condition of the defeated host and the words Satan chooses to describe it, as his flattery depends on the attribution of titles that no longer by divine sanction truly name the fallen angels. He describes the prostration of the host as if they were still in Heaven, with the freedom to choose gentle "repose" or comfortable "slumber" or prayer. The sarcastic tone of this description suggests the absurdity of such language when applied to fallen beings and yet, by ignoring the moral or theological significance of their fall, also asserts Satan's power to impose such words at will. The implication again is that the condition of the angels has no moral or theological meaning in itself. It is a mere neutral fact, not a divinely imposed punishment for sin, and therefore can be described according to the observer's intentions. This assumption of the arbitrariness of words, implied in all Satan's uses of language, is phrased explicitly in one of his taunting replies to Michael during the war in Heaven:[6]

> . . . erre not that so shall end
> The strife which thou call'st evil, but wee style
> The strife of Glorie: which we mean to win,
> Or turn this Heav'n it self into the Hell
> Thou fablest, here however to dwell free,
> If not to reign: mean while thy utmost force,
> And join him nam'd *Almightie* to thy aid,
> I flie not, but have sought thee farr and nigh.
>
> [VI, 288-295]

The words "evil," "Glorie," "Heav'n," and "Hell" can be interchanged at will because they are only neutral names, not definitions of moral or theological qualities or conditions existing independently of the speaker who uses them. Even the name *"Almightie"* is implied to originate in the propagandistic intentions of the enemy rather than in the nature of God, so that by denying Him this "title" Satan claims to take away the omnipotence it defines.

Style, then, is for Satan both a means and a display of power. In his derision of the enemy during the war

in Heaven, when he gloats over their collapse before
gun-fire, his exaggeratedly stylized manner makes his
control over them seem verbal as much as military. He
glories in his effectiveness with words as with arms:

> O Friends, why come not on these Victors proud?
> Ere while they fierce were coming, and when wee,
> To entertain them fair with open Front
> And Brest, (what could we more?) propounded terms
> Of composition, strait they chang'd thir minds,
> Flew off, and into strange vagaries fell,
> As they would dance, yet for a dance they seemd
> Somwhat extravagant and wilde, perhaps
> For joy of offerd peace: but I suppose
> If our proposals once again were heard
> We should compel them to a quick result.
>   [VI, 609-619]

Not only are the words he uses to describe the scene
again willfully inappropriate to what is actually hap-
pening, but his sarcastic tone is also consciously at
variance with his meaning. His boasts are phrased in
urbane social accents: he sounds politely offended by
the "strange vagaries" of his foes, seems to criticize
their manners as "Somwhat extravagant and wilde"
for a ballroom. The tone of this speech (actually an
echo of Patroklos' "bitter mockery" when he describes
a death in battle as the vaulting of an acrobat)[7] has
effects similar to those created elsewhere by Satan's
parodies of literary styles. A comparison is suggested
by this tone with modes of language familiar to us in
the fallen world. The reader hears in Satan's voice a
prediction of a society like the one which is Dryden's
subject. By this device Milton measures Satan's fall

from his original state in Heaven as Dryden, primarily through Miltonic allusion and parody, measures the distance between the archetypal world of *Paradise Lost* and his own corrupt society.

The vicious manipulation of language in Satan's public speeches may be read as an expression (like that in Shakespeare's Roman plays especially) of distrust for political oratory, an issue which certainly concerned Milton, in his role as propagandist for Cromwell's government, as it concerned Dryden, the official poet of the restored royalist party, and all English writers who lived through the upheavals of the seventeenth century. Yet the habits of language which characterize Satan's speeches in the opening scene, during the council and war in Heaven, and at his return to Hell, are evidence of more than the dangerous influence of political intentions upon public language. By the inclusion of soliloquies, Milton is at pains to show that these habits of utterance characterize Satan's speech when he alone can hear it. They are the chief evidence of his fallen condition, which transforms not public ethics alone but the moral fabric of his being.

Our introduction to Eden and to its inhabitants is framed by two soliloquies of Satan. In the first and more famous passage he reviews his plight, acknowledges his despair, and then appears to entertain the notion of repentance:

> O then at last relent: is there no place
> Left for Repentance, none for Pardon left?
> None left but by submission; and that word
> *Disdain* forbids me, and my dread of shame
> Among the Spirits beneath, whom I seduc'd
> With other promises and other vaunts

Then to submit, boasting I could subdue
Th' Omnipotent. Ay me, they little know
How dearly I abide that boast so vaine . . .
[IV, 79-87]

There seems a saving truthfulness, absent from his
public addresses, in this recognition of his own false
oratory. His struggling pride and despair give the soliloquy a special dramatic character. It has some of the
gigantic pathos of Achilles' speeches, evokes something
like the sympathy with which we hear the soliloquies
of Marlowe's Faustus, of Macbeth, or Hamlet. Yet
Satan's private language here seems also designed to
reveal the same lack of connection found in his political
speeches between words and moral or theological meanings existing outside his own mind. He can find no place
for repentance "but by submission; and that word /
Disdain forbids me." Characteristically he thinks of
the "word" as if it were separable from its meaning:
"submission" is a name which he can arbitrarily use
or refuse in describing his relationship to God, and
indeed "submission" has no meaning that he can
understand, nor do words referring to any other moral
or theological qualities or states. "Evil be thou my
Good" [IV, 110] he exclaims, because in his fallen
condition neither "Evil" nor "Good" has referents
outside his own mind, nor is determined by any
power other than his own will. He can change "Evil"
into "Good" by reversing the words themselves, as
the mind can "make a Heav'n of Hell, a Hell of
Heav'n" [I, 255] by asserting its own autonomy.

The soliloquy spoken after Satan's first sight of
Adam and Eve reveals more fully the abuses of language which are his chief instrument in the corruption

of man. Satan speaks to himself as if he were talking to them; even his solitary utterances are framed as if to *persuade,* since language for him has no other use or value. Even alone he postulates an audience:

> . . . League with you I seek,
> And mutual amitie so streight, so close,
> That I with you must dwell, or you with me
> Henceforth; my dwelling haply may not please
> Like this fair Paradise, your sense, yet such
> Accept your Makers work; he gave it me,
> Which I as freely give; Hell shall unfould,
> To entertain you two, her widest Gates,
> And send forth all her Kings; there will be room,
> Not like these narrow limits, to receive
> Your numerous ofspring; if no better place,
> Thank him who puts me loath to this revenge
> On you who wrong me not for him who wrongd.
> And should I at your harmless innocence
> Melt, as I doe, yet public reason just,
> Honour and Empire with revenge enlarg'd,
> By conquering this new World, compels me now
> To do what else though damnd I should abhorre.
>   [IV, 375-392]

The unctuous geniality of the tone is as much at variance with his feelings as the diction predicting our formulas for social invitations is inappropriate to his threats. He seems to take pleasure in this conscious manipulation of language although he alone hears it; even in soliloquy he artfully shapes his style to make it serviceable as a weapon or instrument. To argue his cause though only to himself he invokes "public reason just, / Honour and Empire with revenge enlarg'd," words again referring to no moral or theological meanings that he can understand. By "reason" Satan means merely "purpose" or "cause," which he calls both "just" and "public," implying that it is "just" *because* it is "public," because he and his followers have decided to call it "just." Similarly he detaches the word "Honour" from any meaning independent of his own interest: it is linked instead with "Empire" and "revenge" and therefore reduces to merely another name for what Satan wants, power. His private speech imitates all the abuses of his political oratory; even to himself, as the narrator remarks, he argues the "Tyrants plea" [IV, 394].

Language as dangerous power is represented before the Fall of man in Satan's speeches. It is emphasized by the narrator's interpretations of them, by Raphael's comments upon Satan's "Ambiguous words" [V, 703; VI, 568] and his "calumnious Art/ Of counterfeted truth" [V, 770-771], and by God's prediction that man will fall victim to the Devil's "glozing lyes" [III, 93]. This attention to Satanic modes of language foreshadows the temptation scene, where the divine prediction is specifically recalled in the narrator's comment after the serpent's first speech to Eve:

So gloz'd the Tempter, and his Proem tun'd;
Into the Heart of *Eve* his words made way,
Though at the voice much marveling . . .
[IX, 549-551]

Here and throughout the scene we are made to attend to the artful shaping of Satan's speech and to the power of his words, which seem almost to have life and motion of their own. This emphasis is particularly marked in the extended simile preceding Satan's fateful last speech:

As when of old som Orator renound
In *Athens* or free *Rome,* where Eloquence
Flourishd, since mute, to som great cause addrest,
Stood in himself collected, while each part,
Mótion, each act won audience ere the tongue,
Somtimes in highth began, as no delay
Of Preface brooking through his Zeal of Right.
So standing, moving, or to highth upgrown
The Tempter all impassiond thus began.
                                    [IX, 670-678]

The succeeding speech itself is a parody of a formal
oratorical style[8] and therefore, like other speeches of
Satan which parody literary genres and modes of
language, identifies him as belonging to the fallen
world, into which Eve will gladly follow him. After the
speech the narrator acknowledges its force by again
endowing Satan's words with a serpentine life of their
own:

He ended, and his words replete with guile
Into her heart too easie entrance won:
Fixt on the Fruit she gaz'd, which to behold
Might tempt alone, and in her ears the sound
Yet rung of his perswasive words, impregn'd
With Reason, to her seeming, and with Truth . . .
                                    [IX, 733-738]

The persuasiveness of this oratory is further attested
by Eve herself, who is induced by it to praise the forbidden tree first because it

Gave elocution to the mute, and taught
The Tongue not made for Speech to speak thy praise:
Thy praise hee also who forbids thy use,
Conceales not from us, naming thee the Tree

Of Knowledge, knowledge both of good and evil;
Forbids us then to taste, but his forbidding
Commends thee more, while it inferrs the good
By thee communicated, and our want:
For good unknown, sure is not had, or had
And yet unknown, is as not had at all.

[IX, 748-757]

By "elocution" she means speech, but the redundancy
of the first two lines shows her to mean also calculated
eloquence, artful speech,[9] a distinction revealing that
she has entered the fallen world because she has conceived for the first time of the willful manipulation of
language. Utterance is no longer a divine gift—the
"Tongue not made for Speech" can escape its created
limits—but a function of the will. Her attitude toward
language is now Satan's, exposes the same corruption.
Even to herself (before only Satan soliloquized, for
Adam and Eve in their innocence spoke to each other
as to themselves) she talks as if she were persuading
an audience. Because she interprets language now according to calculated intention—"praise," "forbids,"
"Conceales," "naming," "Forbids," "forbidding,"
"Commends"—she therefore defines moral categories
like "good" as they satisfy self-interest, and the fact
that she does so before she eats the forbidden fruit
finally confirms the power of Satan's language. His
words are the poison that corrupts her; his rhetoric
is the cause of man's Fall.

The dangerous possibilities of language in *Absalom and Achitophel* have more explicitly political implications because of the nature of the poem's occasion.
Yet, as we have seen, by allowing its occasion to be
interpreted among other ways as a modern, local instance of Milton's story, Dryden provides a literary

and moral context which extends its political reference to include the recurring patterns of history in the fallen world. The dangers wrought by language in Restoration politics, as in David's reign, are the dangers always lurking in human society.

Dryden's speaker in his account of the temptation and fall of Absalom directs the reader's attention, like the narrator in *Paradise Lost,* to abuses of language as the source and sign of corruption. Achitophel is portrayed, after the model of Satan, as a master of rhetoric whose false speech is the cause of Absalom's downfall. This parallel is in fact one of the most important means of extending the comparison between Achitophel and Milton's Satan, and therefore between Dryden's satire and *Paradise Lost.* Achitophel's temptations of Absalom are a re-enactment of the seduction by Satan of Eve, the archetypal model of all such scenes which, in Milton's own allusive presentation, is made to include other literary temptations. Dryden's scene in a similar manner mingles echoes of other Biblical and literary seductions (especially the second Adam's temptations by Satan in *Paradise Regained*)[10] within the larger comparison to Book IX of *Paradise Lost.*

Dryden begins to forge the connections between his temptation scene and Milton's in the interpretive comment by the narrator which introduces Achitophel's first speech:

Him he attempts, with studied Arts to please,
And sheds his Venome, in such words as these.
[228-229]

This couplet echoes precisely the comment of Milton's speaker prefacing the first temptation of Eve:

>   . . . he glad
> Of her attention gaind, with Serpent Tongue
> Organic, or impulse of vocal Air,
> His fraudulent temptation thus began.
>   [IX, 528-531]

Achitophel's lines following the introduction extend
the parallel with the scene from *Paradise Lost* because
they are a serious parody of Satan's addresses to Eve,
just as Satan's own speeches parody styles of literature belonging to the fallen world. In Achitophel's first
flattering address, for example, there is the same exaggerated mingling of political and sexual seduction that
lurks in Satan's courtly-love language. Absalom is
praised in these mixed terms:

> Auspicious Prince! at whose Nativity
> Some Royal Planet rul'd the Southern sky;
> Thy longing Countries Darling and Desire . . .
>   [230-232]

These lines parallel Satan's appeal to Eve as "sovran
Mistress" [IX, 532], an epithet implying a social hierarchy and a sexual domination which as yet exist only
in the mind of the tempter:

> Thee all things living gaze on, all things thine
> By gift, and thy Celestial Beautie adore
> With ravishment beheld, there best beheld
> Where universally admir'd . . .   [IX, 539-542]

Most skillfully Achitophel is then made to transform
the original tempter's argument that Eve's beauty be
not wasted on the desert air. Satan's plea establishes
the tradition:

In this enclosure wild, these Beasts among,
Beholders rude, and shallow to discerne
Half what in thee is fair, one man except,
Who sees thee? (and what is one?) who shouldst be
   seen
A Goddess among Gods, ador'd and serv'd
By Angels numberless, thy daily Train.
                                    [IX, 543-548]

This traditional literary persuasion to love has sinister
significance as Satan offers it, because it is an invitation to leave the Garden for an imaginary courtly society that offers power and pre-eminence unknown in the
pastoral world of Eden. Absalom, however, already
belongs to such a society, is already jaded by its praise.
Achitophel's temptation of him must therefore offer a
more sophisticated prize than could lure inexperienced
Eve:[11]

How long wilt thou the general Joy detain;
Starve, and defraud the People of thy Reign?
Content ingloriously to pass thy days
Like one of Vertues Fools that feeds on Praise;
Till thy fresh Glories, which now shine so bright,
Grow Stale and Tarnish with our daily sight.
Believe me, Royal Youth, thy Fruit must be,
Or gather'd Ripe, or rot upon the Tree.
                                    [244-251]

Achitophel, like Satan, borrows a conventional formula
of persuasion from love poetry, and his also in its context is a sinister and cynical offer. The traditional invitation to a young lady to gather the buds or blossoms
of love before time withers their beauty and her own
is turned into a political calculation (such as those of

Shakespeare's Bolingbroke). The threat to Absalom is phrased in language appropriate to an aging lady urged to become a courtesan, and the flowers of love are turned into forbidden fruits which must be snatched unlawfully. The fusion of sexual with political language shows a chaos of values in the world which Achitophel offers to Absalom; it hints at the illicit passions, greed, self-interest rotting the most private relationships as well as public enterprises. It acknowledges that the imaginary world offered by Satan to Eve, which then had no existence outside his own mind, is the actual historical world of Dryden's satire. The means which "effect" Absalom's fall are again words of "Praise" uttered by "Hells dire Agent" [303, 373]. This devious rhetoric poisons Absalom, who shows his corruption, like Eve, first by echoing the language of Milton's Satan [P. L. IV, 58-61]:

> Yet oh that Fate Propitiously Enclind,
> Had rais'd my Birth, or had debas'd my Mind;
> To my large Soul, not all her Treasure lent,
> And then Betray'd it to a mean Descent.
>
> [363-366]

And then, after the fashion of Adam and Eve, he mistakes his fall for soaring flight [367]. The scene in the Garden of Eden, therefore, is made to represent the original of the fall of Absalom, of Monmouth, and of all human beings who have been seduced by sexual or political or literary temptations.

By imitating the use of serious parody, as well as by echoing some of the actual language of the scene, Dryden achieves large effects similar to Milton's. For the adaptation of Miltonic style establishes the resemblance between the events of Dryden's poem and the original Fall as it is enacted in *Paradise Lost,* much as Milton's parodies of poetry and oratory belonging to the fallen world point, as it were, forward to the endless recurrences in future history of the archetypal temptation and sin. Furthermore, the use of parody in presenting the central event of each work again emphasizes strikingly the importance of *style itself* as a moral instrument. At the moment of crisis in each poem the reader is warned that the artful manipulation of words can have fatal power and final significance. We are therefore made to interpret the meaning of the event in the light of the poet's attitude toward language.

The connections between Achitophel and Satan as corrupters of language are even richer and more important in their implications than the effects achieved by the parallel temptation scenes. Achitophel not only uses the original tempter's tools of flattery and fraud; he is also made to express an attitude toward language reminiscent of Satan's in *Paradise Lost,* and to debase words in characteristic ways recalling the modes of speech by which Milton distinguishes Satan's fallen condition. He is therefore presented like Satan as an artful abuser of language, the nature and consequences of his abuse of it envisioned as Milton defines Satanic rhetoric.

Achitophel, after the manner of Satan, exploits language exclusively to *persuade,* as he himself acknowledges in his advice to Absalom. The kind of verbal manipulation he advocates and uses is of course specifically political and propagandistic in intention, like Satan's public addresses, but it reveals a moral corruption extending beyond the expediencies of political success, an attitude which denies any necessary correspondence between words and moral or theological

meanings. Like Satan's, Achitophel's "Arts" of language depend upon a conviction of its arbitrariness:

His faithful Friends, our Jealousies and Fears,
Call *Jebusites;* and *Pharaoh*'s Pentioners:
Whom, when our Fury from his Aid has torn,
He shall be Naked left to publick Scorn.
The next Successor, whom I fear and hate,
My Arts have made Obnoxious to the State;
Turn'd all his Vertues to his Overthrow,
And gain'd our Elders to pronounce a Foe.
His Right, for Sums of necessary Gold,
Shall first be Pawn'd, and afterwards be Sold:
Till time shall Ever-wanting *David* draw,
To pass your doubtfull Title into Law:
If not; the People have a Right Supreme
To make their Kings; for Kings are made for them.
All Empire is no more than Pow'r in Trust,
Which when resum'd, can be no longer Just.
Succession, for the general Good design'd,
In its own wrong a Nation cannot bind:
If altering that, the People can relieve,
Better one Suffer, than a Nation grieve.
The *Jews* well know their power: e'r *Saul* they Chose,
God was their King, and God they durst Depose.
Urge now your Piety, your Filial Name,
A Father's Right, and fear of future Fame;
The publick Good, that Universal Call,
To which even Heav'n Submitted, answers all.
                                                    [397-422]

Achitophel's success consists according to his own confession largely in the manipulation of words: he stirs
his party to "Call" the king's friends by damaging
names, to "'pronounce" him "a Foe," as Satan in his

final temptation of Eve calls God "the Threatner" [IX, 687] which she, fallen, turns into "Our great Forbidder" [IX, 815]. His advice to Absalom is to choose effective names for his motives: "Urge now your Piety, your Filial Name," and especially "The publick Good, that Universal Call." Words like "Law," "Piety," "publick Good" refer to no moral principles or qualities or conditions; they have become mere names, to be imposed according to the intention of the speaker as he imposes definitions without reference to original or authoritatively sanctioned meanings: "All Empire is no more than Pow'r in Trust." The contemptuous formula "no more than" (incidentally a form of definition especially characteristic of Hobbes' style)[12] asserts the power of the speaker to alter traditional meanings at will, simply by the force of his own redefinitions.

The same Satanic theory of language and the same consequent abuse of its power are repeatedly revealed in Achitophel's speeches. He dismisses the question of legal succession by derogatory reference to a "Successive Title, Long, and Dark,/ Drawn from the Mouldy Rolls of *Noah*'s Ark" [301-302], as if the divine sanction for kingship were a quaint antique survival and as if "Title" were merely a word written on a scroll. The contemptuous tone is much like Satan's when he speaks of the Almighty as a "Monarch" who reigns "upheld by old repute,/ Consent or custome" [I, 638-640]. Achitophel reduces principles always to names listed in undifferentiated series as political slogans, like Satan's "public reason just,/ Honour and Empire with revenge" [IV, 389-390]:

All sorts of men by my successful Arts,
Abhorring Kings, estrange their alter'd Hearts

From *David*'s Rule: And 'tis the general Cry,
Religion, Common-wealth, and Liberty.
If you as Champion of the publique Good,
Add to their Arms a Chief of Royal Blood;
What may not *Israel* hope, and what Applause
Might such a General gain by such a Cause?
[289-296]

He advises Absalom to exploit the shifting interpretations that the "general Cry," the "Universal Call"
may give to moral terms, and at the same time to "Proclaim" his own:

Leave the warm People no Considering time;
For then Rebellion may be thought a Crime.
Prevail your self of what Occasion gives,
But try your Title while your Father lives:
And that your Arms may have a fair Pretence,
Proclaim, you take them in the King's Defence...
[459-464]

To reinforce the effect of Achitophel's speeches, the
poet, like Milton's narrator commenting upon Satan,
interprets his political practices for us explicitly as
the abuse of language, the nature of the abuse defined
as Milton distinguishes Satanic rhetoric:

The wish'd occasion of the Plot he takes,
Some Circumstances finds, but more he makes.
By buzzing Emissaries, fills the ears
Of listning Crowds, with Jealosies and Fears
Of Arbitrary Counsels brought to light,
And proves the King himself a *Jebusite*:
Weak Arguments! which yet he knew full well,
Were strong with People easie to Rebell.
[208-215]

His tools are "Arguments" as meaningless and insidious as the "buzzing" of insects, but with a dangerous force that "makes" things happen according to his plans. By verbal manipulation, rather than appeals to evidence, he "proves" what the narrator appears to know is untrue.[13] The bitter irony of the word "proves" underlines the absolute cynicism shaping this kind of rhetoric: even those words by which the truth of other words is judged have lost their meanings. Elsewhere the narrator, in his description of the royal "Progress" staged for Monmouth, concludes that more than spectacle, the manipulation of words without regard to traditionally sanctioned meanings, is Achitophel's most effective instrument:

> *Achitophel* had form'd it, with intent
> To sound the depths, and fathom where it went,
> The Peoples hearts; distinguish Friends from Foes;
> And try their strength, before they came to blows:
> Yet all was colour'd with a smooth pretence
> Of specious love, and duty to their Prince.
> Religion, and Redress of Grievances,
> Two names, that always cheat and always please,
> Are often urg'd; and good King *David*'s life
> Indanger'd by a Brother and a Wife.
> Thus, in a Pageant Show, a Plot is made;
> And Peace it self is War in Masquerade. [741-752]

The word "colour'd," while it describes the pageantry of costume, also refers to the colors of rhetoric, which can depict motives or paint over them in a "smooth pretence," and manipulates "names" for moral values without regard to their meanings. The words "Religion, and Redress of Grievances," listed characteristically without distinctions between them, are not indeed definitions of moral values to Achitophel, but neutral names, which can be given only functional worth as instruments of his will. By cutting words off from any origins but his own intentions, he can apply them anywhere; by rhetorical trickery he can present any act or motive as if it were another, to the destruction of all constant values or meanings. The very fabric of society can then be altered by this vicious abuse of language: "And Peace it self is War in Masquerade," a line inverting Raphael's description of the battle in Heaven, "Warr seem'd a civil Game/ To this uproar" [VI, 677-668].

In his borrowings from Milton's presentation of Satan, Satan's temptation of Eve, man's disobedience and its effects on human nature, Dryden forges even closer parallels between his poem and *Paradise Lost* than by his imitations of heroic style and of psychological portraits or "characters." He continually draws upon the reader's familiarity with Milton's epic, insists on the parallels between the two works, in order to express his own conception of evil, which shows more sympathy with Milton's than could have been predicted from his earlier vulgarization of the epic in *The State of Innocence* or from other modes of Miltonic borrowing in *Absalom and Achitophel*. The power of language used arbitrarily as an instrument of persuasion is the chief threat to morality in Milton's interpretation of the Fall and in Dryden's re-enactment, the temptation of Absalom. The corruption of language when words become neutral names severed from original or authoritatively sanctioned moral meanings is the most powerful effect and sign of sin in each poet's view of experience. Their presentations of the temptation and Fall show this deep similarity in attitude, which made the language of large portions of *Paradise Lost* —what we have called Satanic rhetoric—available to Dryden for his own satiric purposes. Dryden's use of that kind of language, within the total Miltonic context of *Absalom and Achitophel,* likens Milton's understanding of evil to his own, and therefore makes the comparison of his satire with *Paradise Lost* central to the meaning of his poem.

III

THE "ALTERD STILE"
OF FALLEN MEN

Milton's Adam and Eve at the end of Book IX enter the fallen world which until then has existed only in the mind of Satan. Their first sign of kinship with him is the deterioration of their speech, which loses the untroubled simplicity of their original pastoral language; they begin to echo his style and to predict the varied and devious accents of men in the fallen world of history.

In her first soliloquy after she has tasted the forbidden fruit Eve repeats phrases we have earlier heard from Satan: "for inferior who is free?" [IX, 825]. In her first speech to Adam we witness her beginning to shape language with conscious artistry in accordance with her needs, without any necessary correspondence between her words and what they describe. The narrator frames that speech with interpretive comments on the artful manipulation of her language which recall his remarks about Satan as master of rhetoric.

Whereas before the Fall her speeches are characteristically introduced by such simple formulas as "To whom
thus Eve," here her temptation of Adam is introduced
with the warning:

> . . . in her face excuse
> Came Prologue, and Apologie to prompt,
> Which with bland words at will she thus addrest.
>
> [IX, 853-855]

The theatrical metaphor associates her with play-
acting and therefore with Satan who, to tempt her, had
assumed the "part" of indignant sympathizer [IX,
667].[1] Her performance is followed by: "Thus *Eve*
with Countnance blithe her storie told" [IX, 886], the
word "storie" now implying a fiction rather than a
simple account, such as she earlier gave of her creation.
The syntax of her "storie" is suspended with serpentine intricacy, a single sentence weaving itself from
line 861 to line 878, so that the telling of events is constantly interrupted by qualifying explanations quite
absent from her earlier story in Book IV. Her tone also
implies new and more varied shades of feeling appropriate in a more complex and contradictory society
than the pastoral world of Eden. No longer is the adjective "sweet" simply descriptive of her "accent"
[IX, 321], nor does she use it habitually, as before, to
define her experiences. Her final persuasion, for example, is phrased in language more suited to the sophisticated tastes of a court coquette than to the "Harvest
Queen" [IX, 842] for whom Adam had woven the now
fading garland. She tells him what the reader knows
from her earlier self-revelations to be a lie about her
motives for wanting god-head:

> ...which for thee
> Chiefly I sought, without thee can despise.
> For bliss, as thou hast part, to me is bliss,
> Tedious, unshar'd with thee, and odious soon.
> [IX, 877-880]

These lines, with their acknowledgment of time passing, are a painful transformation of her earlier love
poetry, especially the lyric that began "With thee
conversing I forget all time" and ended with inevitable
rightness "nor walk by Moon, / Or glittering Starr-
light without thee is sweet" [IV, 639-656]. In contrast
now to "sweet," she uses such words as "despise,"
"Tedious," "odious," which, with their upperclass
suggestions of bored fastidiousness, have never been
uttered by man in Eden before. They replace the Biblical language, especially the metaphors allowed by the
fact of Eve's creation from Adam's rib, with which she
as well as he habitually defined their union. The presence of such cynical expressions severs a word like
"bliss" from its theological origin, reducing it to mean
the opposite of what is "Tedious," a kind of titillating
pleasure. Eve's tone, a prediction of speech in the society of the fallen world, is therefore, like Satan's characteristically, at variance for the first time with the
moral or theological significance of her now changing
experience.

From the beginning of Eve's soliloquy throughout
Books IX and X, the drama of corruption is acted out
in the progressive degeneration of human language.
The seeds of decay in Eve's first fallen words bloom
into monstrous distortions. Both Adam and Eve not
only echo earlier speeches of Satan, but Adam, in his
new kinship of feeling with the fallen angel, actually

invents and pronounces a speech which he predicts that
Satan will say [IX, 948-950]. Both express themselves,
within their characteristic modes of utterance, in more
contorted sentence structure. The contrast is not between simplicity and complexity of style, but between
transparent language expressing purity of motive, and
devious speech used to disguise intention. If Eve's
style of narration has changed from a simply additive
or sequential "and . . . and . . . when . . . then" construction to the far more complicated syntax of her
persuasive "storie," Adam's natural mode of logical
reasoning also develops in newly elaborate grammati-
cal constructions. His first speech in Book IV, for example, presents an argument for the goodness of God
who has showered man with bountiful gifts but only one
prohibition, the logic of that argument depending on
a single, simple indicative: "needs must the Power /
That made us . . . Be infinitly good" [IV, 412-414].
In contrast, his argument for eating the forbidden
fruit turns upon many complications of logic that mod-
ify, contradict or cancel each other: "But . . . nor . . .
yet so . . . Perhaps . . . perhaps . . . Nor yet . . . yet . . .
cannot be / But . . . Nor can I think that . . . Though
. . . which . . . needs with us must . . . so . . . though . . .
yet . . . least . . . However . . . if . . . So . . . for . . ."
[IX, 926-959]. Poisoned by Eve's serpentine rhetoric,
as she was corrupted by Satan's, Adam reasons in the
intricate confusions of fallen language even before he
has actually tasted the forbidden fruit. Finally, both
express themselves in tones of voice hitherto suggested
only by the range of Satan's speeches. If Eve fastidi-
ously imagines that "bliss" would be "Tedious" without Adam, he, still more viciously, looking back upon
the state of innocence, disdains it in words echoing

Satan's to Eve [IX, 596-597], as dull by comparison
with sin:

> *Eve,* now I see thou art exact of taste,
> And elegant, of Sapience no small part,
> Since to each meaning savour we apply,
> And Palate call judicious; I the praise
> Yeild thee, so well this day thou hast purvey'd.
> Much pleasure we have lost, while we abstain'd
> From this delightful Fruit, nor known till now
> True relish, tasting; if such pleasure be
> In things to us forbidden, it might be wish'd,
> For this one Tree had bin forbidden ten.
> But come, so well refresh't, now let us play,
> As meet is, after such delicious Fare;
> For never did thy Beautie since the day
> I saw thee first and wedded thee, adorn'd
> With all perfections, so enflame my sense
> With ardor to enjoy thee, fairer now
> Then ever, bountie of this vertuous Tree.
>
> [IX, 1017-1033]

The fact that this speech is designed as a *persuasion*
to love, when Adam needed before only to take Eve
by the hand, recalls Satan's parody of love poetry in
his temptation of Eve (and in her dream) and looks
forward to the seduction of Helen by Paris which the
last lines paraphrase.[2] The ugly tone of the speech
is yet another prediction of the fallen world. Having
lost all sense of the origin of the fruit and the moral
significance of eating it, Adam speaks of his experience
in a tone shockingly at variance with its nature. There
is a displeasingly foppish quality to his appreciation
of the forbidden fruit and to his equation of it with
Eve; he talks like a jaded gourmet, in perfect contrast,

for example, with his earlier invitation to Raphael to share the gift of food that God has given to His creatures:

> Heav'nly stranger, please to taste
> These bounties which our Nourisher, from whom
> All perfet good unmeasur'd out, descends,
> To us for food and for delight hath caus'd
> The Earth to yeild; unsavourie food perhaps
> To spiritual Natures; only this I know,
> That one Celestial Father gives to all.
>
> [V, 397-403]

To fallen Adam, both eating and love-making have become titillations of tired senses, not gifts of God but forms of sophisticated "play" like his own talk.

Man's "alterd stile" [IX, 1132], to which the narrator with that phrase draws attention, consists of the same abuses that characterize Satan's language and shows the same corruption of attitude. Adam and Eve have lost their first understanding of the moral or theological meanings of their experiences, and have therefore lost their sense of the necessary correspondence between words and the moral or theological qualities or conditions to which they originally referred. They no longer believe in the theory of language articulated by Abdiel and demonstrated to be true by Adam's power of "rightly" calling the beasts according to their natures, by Eve's instinct to name the flowers [XI, 277]. To fallen man as to Satan, words have become names assigned according to the intentions of the speaker, severed from any roots, arbitrarily interchangeable. In "mutual accusation" [IX, 1187] Adam and Eve make words mean whatever they will.

When "mov'd with touch of blame," Eve renounces the moral terms in which Adam condemns her Fall:[3]

> What words have past thy Lips, *Adam* severe,
> Imput'st thou that to my default, or will
> Of wandering, as thou call'st it, which who knows
> But might as ill have happ'nd thou being by,
> Or to thy self perhaps . . .   [IX, 1144-1148]

Her use of "Imput'st" marks with especial irony the debasing of Eve's language, for she intends it to mean "merely choose to call," as if the power to "impute" meanings were not ultimately God's alone.[4] Adam, "first incenst," in turn rejects the words in which she judges the morality of his act:

> . . . but I rue
> That errour now, which is become my crime,
> And thou th' accuser. Thus it shall befall
> Him who to worth in Women overtrusting
> Lets her Will rule; restraint she will not brook,
> And left to her self, if evil thence ensue,
> Shee first his weak indulgence will accuse.
>   [IX, 1180-1186]

"Default," "errour," "crime," "indulgence" have lost their meanings; their application is now determined by motive alone. Language therefore no longer has the transparency that characterized the talk of unfallen beings. No speaker now simply expresses his meaning by "rightly" discovering names pre-existing in the mind of God. Now language must be interpreted in the light of the speaker's intention, its complications of tone and syntax read as artful means of persuasion (contention being an openly hostile form of persuasion) dependent on flattery, insult, and deception. The dangerous power of Satan's rhetoric has lured Adam and Eve from their pastoral state into a world which no longer exists only in his imagination, a world created now by their own ways of talking. Their conversational exchanges, losing the ritualistic order of pastoral psalms or masques, assume the shape of dialogues in domestic drama familiar in the fallen world, as Satan's speeches, with all their heroic pretense, predict the pattern of political oratory in corrupt human society.

Human society that comes into being in *Paradise Lost* with the Fall of Adam and Eve is the world of history in which all the action of *Absalom and Achitophel* takes place and Dryden, like Milton, defines that society as one in which language has lost its connections with a moral order, has become mere verbal chaos. King David, for example, in his final authoritative proclamation, attributes Absalom's downfall to the power of words which in his own time have been severed from their traditional moral meanings:

> Gull'd with a Patriots name, whose Modern sense
> Is one that would by Law supplant his Prince:
> The peoples Brave, the Politicians Tool;
> Never was Patriot yet, but was a Fool.
>
> [965-968]

Achitophel's success as the tempter who "Gull'd" Absalom depends upon his use of a language to which his contemporaries respond because it is their own. If he is more skillful than others in the manipulation of words, his own diseased rhetoric is a symptom of a more generally prevailing malady. The response

of his listeners to his arbitrary application of names
for moral issues depends, King David's analysis implies, upon some recent agreement or conspiracy to
alter the traditionally sanctioned meanings of words.
This notion is supported by Achitophel's repeated appeals to the "Generall Shout" [60], the "general Cry"
[291], the "Universal Call" [421], the "Common Cry"
[783]—appeals whose efficacy the narrator analyzes
in his portrait of Achitophel:

> Then, seiz'd with Fear, yet still affecting Fame,
> Usurp'd a Patriott's All-attoning Name.
> So easie still it proves in Factious Times,
> With publick Zeal to cancel private Crimes:
> How safe is Treason, and how sacred ill,
> Where none can sin against the Peoples Will...
> [178-183]

"Factious Times" like those of Charles' reign and
David's are responsible for the success of Achitophel's
verbal arts, because traditional values are denied and
therefore words like "Crimes" and "sin" have become
rootless, shifting, and empty, and "Patriott" is the
name for a political party.[5] Morality has been shouted
down by the noise of crowds:

> Nor is the Peoples Judgment always true:
> The most may err as grosly as the few.
> And faultless Kings run down, by Common Cry,
> For Vice, Oppression, and for Tyranny.
> [781-784]

The poet's adjective "faultless" is so confidently in
contradiction to the "Common Cry," with its suggestions of ignorant shouting, that the words expressing

the ideals of the popular party are made to seem as
empty of meaning and as arbitrarily chosen as the
colors for political posters. Speaking of the history
of the Jews just preceding the events of the poem,
the narrator points to political power as the dictator
of moral attitudes, which may be manipulated simply
by the interchange of adjectives:

> But when the chosen people grew more strong,
> The rightfull cause at length became the wrong . . .
>
> [88-89]

The poem's occasion is itself introduced as an
eruption of bad language:

> From hence began that Plot, the Nation's Curse,
> Bad in it self, but represented worse.
>
> [108-109]

Here "Curse" has both the general meaning of
"plague" or "ill-fortune" and the specific significance
of "words spoken as the pronouncement of evil fate."
These words are vicious in themselves, but even more
dangerous in their generative power, that spawns
more words by which the original falsehoods are
further "represented." Bad language is therefore both
cause and effect of the disturbances which the narrator
then describes:

> Rais'd in extremes, and in extremes decry'd;
> With Oaths affirm'd, with dying Vows deny'd.
> Not weigh'd, or winnow'd by the Multitude;
> But swallow'd in the Mass, unchew'd and Crude.
> Some Truth there was, but dash'd and brew'd with
>   Lyes;

To please the Fools, and puzzle all the Wise.
Succeeding times did equal folly call,
Believing nothing, or believing all.

[110-117]

Because neither the speaker of the words, nor their
referents are given, the "Oaths" and "Vows" acquire
a fierce life of their own, tilting at each other in noisy
combat, "Rais'd in extremes" like weapons and "de-
cry'd" with answering violence. This extravagant and
uncritical language is dangerous because it has no necessary correspondence to what it describes; its origins
are in the intentions of politicians who make propa-
ganda out of national disaster:

Some Truth there was, but dash'd and brew'd with
    Lyes;
To please the Fools, and puzzle all the Wise.

[114-115]

By defining the satire's occasion as a verbal upheaval,
the narrator cautions us, like Milton's speaker from
the very beginning of the poem, to be alert in guarding
against persuasive corruptions of language, to contrast
with them his own style which, by its balanced anti-
theses and measured caesuras, opposed itself to the
extravagant and uncritical shouting that these lines
condemn.

Implied also by Dryden's condemnation of chaotic
language in the "modern" world is another sort of
contrast—between language in its deterioration and
words as they were used in their original or earlier
forms, before "The rightfull cause at length became
the wrong" [89]. This implied contrast is of course
supported by the parallels between *Absalom and Achi-*

tophel and *Paradise Lost*. If we are invited to see Achitophel as a Satanic figure, and to read his temptation of Absalom as the re-enactment of the temptation of man, then we see Absalom before his corruption as a representative of unfallen humanity and England's history before these upheavals as a sort of golden age, "While *David,* undisturb'd, in *Sion* raign'd" [42]. The language at the beginning of the satire, as well as the parallels with *Paradise Lost* sustained throughout the poem, seem to support such a contrast between an earlier time and the corrupt modern scene. The decay of words in the fallen world for which Achitophel is spokesman we expect, then, to be measured in the poem by contrast with a once purer language, in the ways that the "alterd stile" of Adam and Eve, like Satan's abuse of words, is contrasted in every detail with speech in the state of innocence, as God according to Abdiel's theory (and Milton's) created it.

These expectations, however, are not fulfilled by the satire, and it is precisely in his ways of thwarting them that Dryden enforces his demonstration of the deceptive power of words. For he plays upon the reader's most sophisticated verbal responses. Assuming a cultivated knowledge of literature, which will encourage in us traditional associations with certain uses of language, he then leads us to recognize the uncritical predictability of those associations. Assuming also in his audience the capacity to appreciate witty word play, to discern the implications of social and sexual innuendo, he then aims his joking in unexpected directions which make our first enjoyment of it seem as uncritical as our too ready responses to traditional literary associations. By arousing and then baffling our expectations in these ways, Dryden allows turns in his narrator's argument which show the need to guard against the dangerous deceptiveness of language, and which at the same time enrich our sense of the speaker's verbal powers.

The satire begins with a description of an earlier time, far distant from the present, which has been revealed to the poet in Scripture:

> In pious times, e'r Priest-craft did begin,
> Before *Polygamy* was made a sin;
> When man, on many, multiply'd his kind,
> E'r one to one was, cursedly, confind:
> When Nature prompted, and no law deny'd
> Promiscuous use of Concubine and Bride;
> Then, *Israel's* Monarch, after Heaven's own heart,
> His vigorous warmth did, variously, impart
> To Wives and Slaves: And, wide as his Command,
> Scatter'd his Maker's Image through the Land.
>
> [1-10]

The line "E'r one to one was, cursedly, confind" wittily identifies the "pious times" of David's reign as a kind of pre-fallen world, for the word "cursedly" is both a polite oath of the sort used in modern society about such tiresome attitudes as sexual prudery, and an allusion to the curse pronounced on fallen Adam, to which the speaker refers as if its effects had not yet been felt.[6] There are also playful echoes of pastoral language in this description, identifying the world of David's reign as a simpler society, without "Priest-craft" or "law," acting spontaneously according to the promptings of "Nature." A kind of cheerful innocence (readily recognizable as the invention of sophisticated wit) characterizes the terms used for behavior in this world: what later times call "sin" could then be described as "vigorous warmth"; what the present condemns even in kings as "Promiscuous use" was then generously interpreted as scattering "his Maker's Image through the Land." The equation of David's reign with an age of innocence is further supported by the description of Absalom, the finest fruit of Nature's prompting:

> Of all this Numerous Progeny was none
> So Beautifull, so brave as *Absolon*:
> Whether, inspir'd by some diviner Lust,
> His Father got him with a greater Gust;
> Or that his Conscious destiny made way
> By manly beauty to Imperiall sway.
> Early in Foreign fields he won Renown,
> With Kings and States ally'd to *Israel*'s Crown:
> In Peace the thoughts of War he coud remove,
> And seem'd as he were only born for love.
> What e'r he did was done with so much ease,
> In him alone, 'twas Natural to please.
> His motions all accompanied with grace;
> And *Paradise* was open'd in his face.
>
> [17-30]

The hero of this unfallen world is a "Natural" man identified by "Natural" qualities which are described, with the same sort of wittily disguised sexual innuendo, in terms recalling the cheerful and innocent abundance of life associated in the first passage with a golden age or earthly paradise, whose lovely image "open'd in his face." The description also specifically echoes Milton's language about unfallen Adam, whose "manly beauty" is characteristically described as "grace," marking both the divine origin and the theological or moral significance of his nature.

This world presented at the opening of the poem would seem to be defined, through its Biblical and pastoral associations, as a contrast with the chaotic society created by the devilish Achitophel and his followers, where David can no longer reign "undisturb'd." The description would, then, like Milton's early scenes in Eden, provide a source of contrasts with fallen experience as it is known to the readers of the poem and as it grows familiar to the unfallen characters when they have succumbed to the persuasions of the Devil. Yet even in these opening passages of the satire there are hints of danger to be found in a world of "Nature" unconfined by "law," and in the "Natural" man inhabiting it.[7] For example, "Scatter'd his Maker's Image through the Land" combines the figure of a monarch distributing *largesse* with the pastoral image of a rustic sowing seed which he will duly harvest in abundance, but in the political context of "wide as his Command," the word "Scatter'd" hints at a kind of willful carelessness or waste, a disorder in the planting which promises no full harvest. This hint in turn modifies our response to the word "undisturb'd," which takes on the added meaning of "inattentive." Or in the description of Absalom, the phrase "Natural to please" implies a kind of indiscriminateness, perhaps even a fawning quality recalling the serpent as it appeared to Eve: "pleasing was his shape, / And lovely" [IX, 503-504]. The suggestion that Paradise was "open'd" in his face warns at least of vulnerability to lurking danger if not eagerness to receive it. Such hints grow louder and more ominous in the last lines of Absalom's portrait:

Some warm excesses, which the Law forbore,
Were constru'd Youth that purg'd by boyling o'r:
And *Amnon*'s Murther, by a specious Name,
Was call'd a Just Revenge for injur'd Fame.
Thus Prais'd, and Lov'd, the Noble Youth remain'd,
While *David,* undisturb'd, in *Sion* raign'd.

[37-42]

"Warm excesses" resembles David's "vigorous warmth," both phrases seeming to claim a healthy innocence for these illegal acts. Yet the danger of such natural promptings is implied by the metaphor of purging which identifies Absalom's nature as a diseased state that overflows violently like a flood, the first of many images in the satire likening the events it describes to disorders in nature such as enter the world after the Fall [136-141, 785-790, 926]. The last lines of the portrait may be partly ambiguous: "Thus Prais'd, and Lov'd" claims nothing of Absalom's worth, but merely suggests a passing reputation. There is, however, no ambiguity at all in the accusation of "Murther" or—especially because throughout the satire moral corruption is distinguished by arbitrary uses of language—in the contrast between the poet's choice of that word "Murther" and the flattering term "Just Revenge" which Absalom's political supporters "call'd" it, as they tactfully "constru'd" his illegal acts to be "Youth . . . boyling o'r."

We have therefore been misled by our associations with the Biblical and especially the Miltonic language in these passages, to read the description of the "pious times" of David's reign as a pastoral, to see "old *Jerusalem*" as a golden age or earthly paradise and Absalom as the representative of unfallen innocence. Looking back at these lines we can see that the poet has actually claimed very few differences between these "pious times" and the present. People behaved then much as they have since: what is said of King David applies as aptly to King Charles. The only difference was that they, having no "Priest-craft," had no laws defining categories of "sin." [8] Their legal and moral terminology was therefore simpler, but that greater simplicity, while it may imply indulgent allowance for nature's promptings, is not therefore a synonym for innocence. For "Nature" itself is not innocent, as we are explicitly warned, first by the accusation of Absalom, the "Natural" man, as a murderer, and throughout the poem by still other passages associating the "Natural" state with violence and disorder. As prelude to Achitophel's choice of Absalom for rebel leader, the narrator remarks on the course of history:

Weak Arguments! which yet he knew full well,
Were strong with People easie to Rebell.
For, govern'd by the *Moon,* the giddy *Jews*
Tread the same track when she the Prime renews:
And once in twenty Years, their Scribes Record,
By natural Instinct they change their Lord.

[214-219]

"Natural Instinct" in man is equated with the fickle power of the moon, with shifting tides and hence with floods which boil over their proper confines like Absalom's "Youth." The revolutions of history recur as relentlessly as the phases of the moon, as dangerously as flood tides, because "natural Instinct" remains as an abiding threat to order.

Such anti-pastoral notions appear in virtually every description of the Jews, intensifying the threats of danger lurking in the opening lines:

These *Adam*-wits, too fortunately free,
Began to dream they wanted libertie;
And when no rule, no president was found
Of men, by Laws less circumscrib'd and bound,
They led their wild desires to Woods and Caves,
And thought that all but Savages were Slaves.

[51-56]

Again Biblical and especially Miltonic allusions lead us to identify the Jews as "*Adam*-wits" with humanity in its "natural" state, but again our associations of "natural" with idealized pastoral man, with unfallen man, are denied or criticized, here actually by means of a specific Miltonic allusion. For the particular passage from *Paradise Lost* echoed in these lines is spoken by Adam at the bitter moment when he discovers that he has lost his innocence and is therefore banished from the pastoral world:

O might I here
In solitude live savage, in some glade
Obscur'd, where highest Woods impenetrable
To Starr or Sun-light, spread thir umbrage broad,
And brown as Evening . . .

[IX, 1084-1088]

In Milton's poem, this corruption of the pastoral world into savagery after the Fall is then marked by the narrator who, alluding to Amazonian jungles, compares Adam and Eve to the "*American*" lately found by Columbus, "girt / With featherd Cincture, naked else and wilde" [IX, 1116-1117], an image of uncivilized man which is not an idealized figure. The effect of the precise Miltonic echo in Dryden's lines is therefore to destroy our Biblical and pastoral associations of natural desires with original innocence. The allusion is a further reminder of the "savage" reality behind the literary idealizations of pastoral poetry, behind the genial indulgence toward nature's promptings in the satire's first lines, behind the "manly beauty" and "pleasing motions" of Absalom. It is to these *"Adam*-wits" that he is a hero because he both shares and appeals to the disordered state which makes them *"Adam*-wits":

> Surrounded thus with Freinds of every sort,
> Deluded *Absalom,* forsakes the Court:
> Impatient of high hopes, urg'd with renown,
> And Fir'd with near possession of a Crown:
> Th' admiring Croud are dazled with surprize,
> And on his goodly person feed their eyes:
> His joy conceal'd, he sets himself to show;
> On each side bowing popularly low:
> His looks, his gestures, and his words he frames,
> And with familiar ease repeats their Names.
> Thus, form'd by Nature, furnish'd out with Arts,
> He glides unfelt into their secret hearts:
> Then with a kind compassionating look,
> And sighs, bespeaking pity ere he spoak,
> Few words he said; but easy those and fit:
> More slow than Hybla drops, and far more sweet.
>   [682-697]

The "Arts" of a politician are not seen, as in Milton's portrait of Satan, to be instrumental in corrupting the gifts of "Nature," but to be a means of enhancing and exploiting them. These gifts have dangerously formed Absalom after the pattern of Achitophel and therefore originally of the Devil himself. Following the promptings of his "Nature," Absalom in turn becomes a serpentine tempter who "glides unfelt" into the corruptible hearts of men, using words like Eve's "far more sweet" than honey, or like Belial's, whose "Tongue / Dropt Manna, and could make the worse appear / The better reason" [II, 112-114]. The consequences for history, as far-reaching as those let loose by Satan's persuasion of Eve and hers of Adam, are described by characteristic comparisons with such disasters as Michael showed to Adam in his prevision of the fallen world:[9]

What Standard is there in the fickle rout,
Which, flowing to the mark, runs faster out?
Nor only Crowds, but Sanhedrins may be
Infected with this publick Lunacy:
And Share the madness of Rebellious times,
To Murther Monarchs for Imagin'd crimes.
If they may Give and Take when e'r they please,
Not Kings alone, (the Godheads Images,)
But Government it self at length must fall
To Natures state; where all have Right to all.
[785-794]

One need not recognize the reference in the last line to Hobbes' definition of the state of nature[10] to read this prediction as a vehement denial of pastoral attitudes, here denounced as irresponsible fantasies. "Natures state" in Dryden's satiric view is not a golden age, but chaos, where terms like "Right" have no moral or theological meanings, are simply other names for power. Our original condition is therefore no different from the disordered present: we are by our very *nature* "byast."

The story from Genesis provides Dryden in *Absalom and Achitophel* with metaphors for states of feeling (longing for power or susceptibility to praise, for instance) and especially for the patterns of political upheaval familiar to seventeenth-century Englishmen;[11] but in his thinking these metaphors have no roots, as they have for Milton, in a comprehensive psychology, theology, and theory of history for which the Fall from original innocence is the supreme and seminal fact. This is not to say that Dryden was theologically unorthodox, but that his formal belief in man's Fall from innocence was not conceived with the imaginative conviction that would make it useful for poetry. The contrast between earlier "pious times" and the disordered present which the poet's witty manipulation of Biblical and pastoral language misleads us to see, turns into a bitter joke. There is in *Absalom and Achitophel* no Eden from which we have strayed, no natural innocence we have corrupted. There is therefore in Dryden's satiric view no Fall of man, no ideal of original purity with which viciousness is contrasted: there are only shifts in terms for human experience which itself remains forever the same.[12]

Absalom and Achitophel read in comparison with *Paradise Lost* reinterprets Milton's story in ways which are predicted in *The State of Innocence* and suggested by the character of Dryden's early writing. In the opera he in no way idealizes unfallen Adam and Eve. He transposes speeches from *Paradise Lost* spoken after they have eaten the forbidden fruit to scenes that take place before the temptation, and allows them unfallen to express vanity, suspicion, jealousy, fear, lust, disappointment—a variety of feelings appropriate to romance, satire, and farce rather than to the pastoral mode that Milton, fusing Biblical and classical traditions, designed for his early scenes in Eden. Whether this sort of revision was a conscious reinterpretation of *Paradise Lost* or a clumsy attempt to make the material presentable on a stage, the unresponsiveness if not hostility to pastoralism (as an ideal) in the opera is consistent with the character of Dryden's other early writings. Except for one or two perfunctory allusions to the pastoral tradition,[13] Dryden largely ignored that mode in his early work, although he wrote in an age still familiar with the notion that a young author should apprentice himself to poetry (as did Spenser and Milton in imitation especially of Virgil and Petrarch) by practicing forms of pastoral verse, and although he alluded to Virgil's *Eclogues* in particular even in his first poetic efforts.[14] Consistently a distrust of pastoral idealization, perhaps a deeply rooted feeling if not a consciously articulated attitude, informs his dramatized adaptation of *Paradise Lost*. He makes no distinction between the created nature of Adam and Eve and their condition after the Fall except the distinction of their ignorance, especially their ignorance of moral terminology. The first dialogue between Adam and newly created Eve coyly acts out this distinction:

> *Adam.*   Made to command, thus freely I obey,
> And at thy feet the whole creation lay.
> Pity that love thy beauty does beget;
> What more I shall desire, I know not yet.
> First let us locked in close embraces be,
> Thence I, perhaps, may teach myself and thee.
>
> *Eve.*   Somewhat forbids me, which I cannot name;
> For, ignorant of guilt, I fear not shame:
> But some restraining thought, I know not why,
> Tells me, you long should beg, I long deny.
> [II, ii, p. 140]

The contrast with Milton's Eve "nor uninformd / Of nuptial Sanctitie and marriage Rites" [VIII, 486-487] could scarcely be louder. In another passage, spoken before she is tempted to sin, Dryden's Eve describes passion in language echoing Milton's description of lust after the Fall [IX, 1029-1050]. Her feelings are not to be distinguished from sexual experience since our loss of innocence. Only her vocabulary is simpler, more limited; she lacks words to describe sensations she cannot explain:

> *Eve.* When your kind eyes looked languishing
> on mine,
> And wreathing arms did soft embraces join,
> A doubtful trembling seized me first all o'er;
> Then, wishes; and a warmth unknown before:
> What followed was all ecstasy and trance;
> Immortal pleasures round my swimming eyes did
> dance,
> And speechless joys, in whose sweet tumult tost,
> I thought my breath and my new being lost.
> [III, i, p. 143]

As in his earlier revision of Shakespeare's *The Tempest* (written in collaboration with Davenant in 1667), Dryden transposes the ideal of pastoral innocence into an image of prurient ignorance.[15] His newly created Adam and Eve, like the citizens of King David's "pious times," differ from their fallen descendants only in the vocabulary they command to describe acts and feelings, to name moral qualities and conditions, common to the "byast Nature" of all men.

The language in such passages of *The State of Innocence* is so clumsy, the feeling so extraordinarily gross, that we tend to dismiss the writing as without interest. Yet such vulgarizations of *Paradise Lost* in the opera are suggestive as they point toward Dryden's later uses of Milton. Attitudes which there often seem to be merely unconscious and uncontrolled misunderstandings of Milton in the later poem become part of a carefully shaped interpretation.

The uses of *Paradise Lost* in *Absalom and Achitophel* show the satire to be conceived by an imagination which shares Milton's definition of experience in the fallen world as the loss of connection between words and necessary or authoritatively sanctioned moral or theological meanings. Dryden, however, gives new emphasis and significance to this definition by consciously and consistently denying any originally pure state from which our present condition is a deterioration; he uses the Fall as a metaphor for patterns of psychological and political experiences without conceiving of it with imaginative conviction as an historical fact. While he could therefore in *Absalom and Achitophel* adapt to his own view Milton's language where it concerned fallen beings, those portions of *Paradise Lost* which recreate Milton's imagining of the original state of innocence were unavailable to Dryden except as targets for the kind of anti-pastoral criticism that informs his presentation of the "Natural" state of man. Contrary to our expectations, which the poet wittily demonstrates to be unguarded, the destructive language of "modern" society cannot therefore be convincingly contrasted in *Absalom and Achitophel* with words in an originally pure, creative form, as in *Paradise Lost* the speech of Satan and fallen man is contrasted in detail with the language of unfallen beings, used as it was divinely intended. So that if society as Dryden portrays it is to be rescued from its present verbal and therefore moral chaos, that recovery cannot be accomplished by language *restored* according to divine intention as, we shall see, words regain their creative force in *Paradise Lost*. If, then, in Dryden's view language has any power to impose order on the chaos of "modern" verbal abuses, its efficacy must have a different source from the restorative gift of eloquence as Milton conceives it in *Paradise Lost*.

IV

THE RESTORATIVE POWER
OF ELOQUENCE

Paradise Lost and *Absalom and Achitophel* both focus upon a human situation which is presented as a paradigm of all man's experiences. The drama of Adam and Eve in the Garden is both the cause and the archetypal image of all human history. The temptation of Absalom by Achitophel and its effects upon their society is a re-enactment of the story of our first parents and therefore an illustration of the recurring patterns of human life. The representative action in both poems includes a temptation, wrought by language willfully abused as an instrument of persuasion, and a fall, whose effects are also shown chiefly as the abuse of words. In both poems the experiences of temptation and loss are ultimately succeeded by a recovery, achieved through the power of utterance, but used creatively as the instrument and the expression of moral order. To give their poems this shape and interpretation, therefore, Milton and Dryden had to demonstrate more than the destructive force of language; they needed also to show the efficacy of language in the restoration of man.

Man's nature is defined in *Paradise Lost* by the special gift of speech, which separates him from the "Quire/ Of Creatures wanting voice" [IX, 198-199], and likens him to the angels, and to God whose "Omnific Word" [VII, 217] made the Book of Works in which man and his language are creatures.[1] This is a perfectly traditional way of defining human nature, but one to which Milton gives especial emphasis. For example, he invents as the first human action Adam's attempt to have a conversation with the other creatures in the landscape, which "answer none return'd" [VIII, 285]. He allows Eve to comment at length on the serpent's ability to articulate the "Language of Man" [IX, 553-563]. With greater elaboration, he shapes the somewhat enigmatic Biblical episode of naming the animals and seeking a help meet for Adam into a "celestial Colloquie sublime" [VIII, 455] on the power of speech. There Adam not only demonstrates his understanding of the lower orders of being in naming them "rightly," but correctly defines Man by his desire for "conversation," for "Social communication" [VIII, 418, 429] which God does not need and which the beasts cannot attain:

I by conversing cannot these erect
From prone, nor in their wayes complacence find.
[VIII, 432-433]

This comment allows for more than its ironic foreshadowing of the temptation scene when Eve finds "complacence" in conversing with the serpent "erect/ From prone"; it enables Adam to demonstrate his unfallen appreciation of speech as the distinguishing power of his nature, the evidence of his rationality. For this understanding he is praised by the "gratious voice Divine":

> Thus farr to try thee, *Adam,* I was pleas'd,
> And finde thee knowing not of Beasts alone,
> Which thou hast rightly nam'd, but of thy self,
> Expressing well the spirit within thee free,
> My Image, not imparted to the Brute . . .
>   [VIII, 437-441]

The gift of "Expressing well" is remarked again and again in unfallen man. Like the angelic choirs, Adam and Eve are repeatedly shown as makers of hymns [IV, 724-735; V, 153-208; IX, 198-199] praised by the poet for literary style as well as for sincerity:

> Lowly they bow'd adoring, and began
> Thir Orisons, each Morning duly paid
> In various style, for neither various style
> Nor holy rapture wanted they to praise
> Thir Maker, in fit strains pronounc't or sung
> Unmeditated, such prompt eloquence
> Flowd from thir lips, in Prose or numerous Verse,
> More tuneable then needed Lute or Harp
> To add more sweetness . . .   [V, 144-152]

Such lines have more important uses than to announce Milton's dislike of liturgical worship, for they contribute to the emphasis on speech, especially on "eloquence" as God's gift to man. This is also made the subject of a dialogue between Raphael and Adam which does not significantly further Adam's education in proper human behavior nor instruct him newly in the works of God, but which seems designed rather to repeat Milton's point about the divine origin of eloquence. When the angel has completed his lessons, Adam offers to tell his own "Storie" because he wishes to detain his guest in order to hear him "reply":

For while I sit with thee, I seem in Heav'n,
And sweeter thy discourse is to my eare
Then Fruits of Palm-tree pleasantest to thirst
And hunger both, from labour, at the houre
Of sweet repast; they satiate, and soon fill,
Though pleasant, but thy words with Grace Divine
Imbu'd, bring to thir sweetness no satietie.
   To whom thus *Raphael* answer'd heav'nly meek.
Nor are thy lips ungraceful, Sire of men,
Nor tongue ineloquent; for God on thee
Abundantly his gifts hath also pour'd
Inward and outward both, his image faire:
Speaking or mute all comliness and grace
Attends thee, and each word, each motion formes.
. . . .
But thy relation now; for I attend,
Pleas'd with thy words no less then thou with mine.
             [VIII, 210-223, 247-248]

Adam's comparison of the "sweetness" of words to fruits, by relating this dialogue to other passages in which food, eating, digestion are the subject, extends the likenesses between men and angels, who can participate in the communion of meals and conversations. It therefore underlines the alternatives open to Adam, who may continue to resemble the unfallen angels in his use of God's gifts, or may learn to abuse them after the example of Satan. The comparison of words to food—suggesting the harmony in unfallen creatures between body and mind, both nourished by the divine gifts—emphasizes speech or conversation as essential sustenance to rational creatures. "Talk" is "Food of the mind," as Adam later argues to dissuade Eve from leaving his company [IX, 238]. Above all, Adam's comparison, and this dialogue as a whole, insists on the special power of language with which God has endowed the rational orders. The angel's words have the substantiality of physical objects but the permanence and illimitability of spirit. They are like fruits, the creations of God, but a fuller, more satisfying revelation of His bounty. Their "sweetness" is the sweetness of eloquence, eloquence the fullest expression of grace, with something of its mysterious power. For Adam, while he listens to the angel, feels himself transported to Heaven, as earlier Raphael's account of the creation seems to cast a kind of magic spell over his listener :[2]

> The Angel ended, and in *Adams* Eare
> So Charming left his voice, that he a while
> Thought him still speaking, still stood fixt to hear;
> Then as new wak't thus gratefully repli'd.
>   [VIII, 1-4]

Eloquence inspired with grace has this effect of visionary inspiration, which informs angelic utterance and the "Unmeditated" hymns and "sweet converse" of unfallen man.

The degeneration of man after the temptation of Eve, as we have seen, is acted out in the decay of human language. Loss of innocence is the loss of creative eloquence which depended on the recognition of the divine origin of language. It is therefore the betrayal of the gift shared by man with the angels, a

betrayal linking him with Satan to the lower orders
that lack the power of utterance. Man's recognition
of his loss of innocence is, then, fittingly marked by
loss of speech:

> ... silent, and in face
> Confounded long they sate, as struck'n mute . . .
> [IX, 1063-1064]

The "sweet converse" for which marriage was established is turned to "vain contest" [IX, 1189], the
form of dialogue typical of literature portraying
matrimony in the fallen world. Biblical pastoral is
replaced by a kind of domestic drama, sometimes
tragic but sometimes almost farcical as insults, self-
justification, and wrangling are exaggerated in the
human conversations following the Fall.[3]

It is the creative power of God's word and the
gift of human eloquence restored which arrest man's
movement downward, following Satan, toward "Eternal silence" [VI, 385], the doom of the fallen angels.
The theological source in the poem for this restorative
process is the utterance of God:

> O Father, gracious was that word which clos'd
> Thy sovran sentence, that Man should find grace;
> For which both Heav'n and Earth shall high extoll
> Thy praises, with th' innumerable sound
> Of Hymns and sacred Songs, wherewith thy Throne
> Encompass'd shall resound thee ever blest.
> [III, 144-149]

The human instrument for this restoration in the
drama of the Fall is the eloquence of Eve. It is she

who interrupts the "sad discourse, and various plaint" [X, 343] into which human conversation has deteriorated, with an effective speech of reconciliation and love.

The turning point in the movement of man toward eternal oblivion comes after we witness Satan's downward passage to Hell and his degeneration into the inarticulate brute serpent. The pastoral world has been transformed into savagery, like the state of "Nature" unconfined by law as Dryden imagines it,[4] where "Beast now with Beast gan war" [X, 710], and Adam's hiding place in "gloomiest shade" [X, 716] resembles Hell as it is first described [I, 244]. In his lament he acknowledges his kinship with the damned: "To *Satan* onely like both crime and doom" [X, 841], and his own language echoes Satan's soliloquy of Book IV. Adam now voices the same despair:

O Conscience, into what Abyss of fears
And horrors hast thou driv'n me; out of which
I find no way, from deep to deeper plung'd!
[X, 842-844]

His fall toward the "Abyss" is marked by his abuse of speech for "complaint" (X, 719) rather than glorification:

O Woods, O Fountains, Hillocks, Dales and Bowrs,
With other echo late I taught your Shades
To answer, and resound farr other Song.
[X, 860-863]

This lament of Adam's for his own "alterd stile"— pastoral hymns or psalms have turned into elegies— is interrupted by Eve's first redemptive motion:

Whom thus afflicted when sad *Eve* beheld,
Desolate where she sate, approaching nigh,
Soft words to his fierce passion she assay'd . . .
[X, 863-865]

The adjective "Soft," with its implications of new
compassion and vulnerability, is especially moving
here, for it has replaced the expected epithet "sweet,"
associated we have seen consistently, almost ritual-
istically, with Eve before the Fall and her "converse"
with Adam. His repulsion of Eve's gesture makes such
"Soft words" seem at first wholly ineffectual:

Out of my sight, thou Serpent, that name best
Befits thee with him leagu'd, thy self as false
And hateful . . .   [X, 867-869]

By changing her God-given title—"Woman" [VIII,
496]—Adam shows forgetfulness of the divine origin
of language and therefore of the moral or theological
meanings which such names were created to define: he
no longer "rightly" names Eve as part of himself,
nor recognizes her place in the Book of God's Works.
In the long tirade which follows he rehearses every
blasphemy heard earlier from Satan. His movement
toward "Eternal silence" appears irreversible: man is
damned and Eden is Hell.

This is the moment chosen for Eve's effective
intervention, in words which precisely echo Christ's
sacrificial offering [III, 227-265] :[5]

Forsake me not thus, *Adam*, witness Heav'n
What love sincere, and reverence in my heart
I beare thee, and unweeting have offended,
Unhappilie deceav'd; thy suppliant

I beg, and clasp thy knees; bereave me not,
Whereon I live, thy gentle looks, thy aid,
Thy counsel in this uttermost distress,
My onely strength and stay: forlorn of thee,
Wither shall I betake me, where subsist?
While yet we live, scarse one short hour perhaps,
Between us two let there be peace, both joyning,
As joyn'd in injuries, one enmitie
Against a Foe by doom express assign'd us,
That cruel Serpent: On me exercise not
Thy hatred for this miserie befall'n.
On me already lost, mee then thy self
More miserable; both have sin'd, but thou
Against God onely, I against God and thee,
And to the place of judgement will return,
There with my cries importune Heaven, that all
The sentence from thy head remov'd may light
On me, sole cause to thee of all this woe,
Mee mee onely just object of his ire.   [X, 914-936]

Not only the close parallel with Christ's speech, but
the thickly woven texture of allusions to earlier, unfallen uses of language, creates the effect of words
restored to something like the purity of man's first
style. Adam, as well as the reader, feels their force:

She ended weeping, and her lowlie plight,
Immoveable till peace obtain'd from fault
Acknowledg'd and deplor'd, in *Adam* wraught
Commiseration; soon his heart relented
Towards her, his life so late and sole delight,
Now at his feet submissive in distress,
Creature so faire his reconcilement seeking,
His counsel whom she had displeas'd, his aide;

As one disarm'd, his anger all he lost,
And thus with peaceful words uprais'd her soon.

[X, 937-946]

The effect of Eve's "plaint" is the effect of grace,
sudden and overpowering. Adam's "heart relented":
he is converted. His own speech becomes "peaceful"—
like Eve he will "no more contend, nor blame" [X, 958]
—as he returns to expressions that characterized his
style before the Fall. Eve is no longer a serpent but
his "sole delight," an echo of the first words he speaks
to her in the poem: "Sole partner and sole part of all
these joyes" [IV, 411]. The movement of restoration in human experience has begun, tending away
from the "Abyss" and upward to Heaven, where fly the
"mute" supplications of Adam and Eve, as yet "Un-
skilful with what words to pray" [XI, 32] because their
accustomed hymns of praise have now turned to con-
fessions.[6]

In the opening of Book XI Milton is careful to
repeat the orthodox theological doctrine, enunciated
earlier by God to Christ [III, 174], that this motion in
the heart of man has been initiated by "Prevenient
Grace descending" from the "Mercie-seat above"
[XI, 2-3]. But because he postpones this repetition of
the doctrinal explanation until after Eve's redemptive
gesture and Adam's conversion, Milton encourages us
to conceive of the turning point of the drama first in
human terms. The instrument of redemption is language purified of Satanic abuses and restored to its
creative eloquence. The "Soft words" of Eve are the
human expression of the Word of her divine Author.
It is she who first leads Adam away from the "Abyss"
with a motion which feels dramatically right: her

speech has believable power to convert Adam. Yet the question remains why Milton chose to make Eve's words the human instrument of redemption when it was she who appeared most susceptible to Satanic rhetoric and when it was Adam who was created to be the "guide" and "head" of mankind.[7]

In the theology of *Paradise Lost,* as of Genesis and traditional interpretations of it, Adam and Eve are to be thought of together as Man, their individual motives for disobedience and their separately pronounced punishments to be understood as the sin and consequent doom of united mankind. In his poetic representation of them, Milton further directs us to think of Adam and Eve as inseparable parts of one soul, especially by his elaborate use of the Biblical Adam's declaration:[8]

. . . This is now bone of my bones, and flesh of my flesh: she shall be called Woman, because she was taken out of man.

Therefore shall a man leave his father and his mother, and shall cleave unto his wife: and they shall be one flesh.   [Genesis ii: 23-24]

When Milton makes Eve the author of the first redemptive speech after the Fall, he is therefore certainly not making a distinction between the effects of sin on female and male natures. He can in one sense be understood to mean that humanity's original condition, though impaired by the Fall, was not irrevocably corrupted like Satan's angelic nature, that within Man's soul (represented by Adam and Eve together) remained traces of his divinely created powers which could still respond to the motions of grace.[9] Yet within the terms of the human drama of sin as it is acted out in the presentation of Adam and Eve after the Fall, we inevitably read the first redemptive speech as the invention of Eve rather than of Adam.

Milton prepares the reader elaborately to make this distinction, and his decision was a calculated one, not dictated by the phrasing of Genesis itself. Only in the Biblical account of the confrontation with God in the Garden is there any hint of a distinction in their feelings of guilt, when Adam is prompt to blame "The woman whom thou gavest to be with me, she gave me of the tree, and I did eat" while Eve says more simply, "The serpent beguiled me, and I did eat" [Genesis iii: 12, 13]. Milton builds carefully to his own dramatization of that scene in the dialogues of Book IX. Adam is the first to break the silence of conscious shame with an accusation of Eve [1067ff] and after they have covered their nakedness it is Adam again accusing who starts the first quarrel [1134ff]. Eve answers in the same manner, however, and it is not until their appearance before the Judge that her feelings are shown in favorable contrast to Adam's arguments. The narrator points out the difference in the introduction of the scene: "He came, and with him *Eve,* more loth, though first/ To offend" [X, 109-110], and Milton's further elaboration of the passage from Genesis seems shaped to emphasize this contrast. He expands the Biblical Adam's speech into an almost farcically exaggerated self-justification, in which Adam pleads Satan's excuse of "strict necessitie" and finally accuses not only Eve for tempting him but God for creating her capable of deception [X, 125-143]. His lies, confusions, and blasphemies are expressed in tortuously qualified and suspended syntax that contrasts with the touching simplicity of Eve's speech,

left by Milton in its Biblical brevity. The difference is
emphasized by the narrator's comment when the Judge
has questioned her:

> To whom sad *Eve* with shame nigh overwhelm'd,
> Confessing soon, yet not before her Judge
> Bold or loquacious, thus abasht repli'd.
> The Serpent me beguil'd and I did eate.
> [X, 159-162]

This contrast between Eve's rightness of feeling and
Adam's corrupted reasoning is further developed after
their judgments are pronounced, in the soliloquy of
Adam, which shows even more tellingly his incapacity
for rational thought. All his arguments lead to a conclusion precisely echoing the narrator's earlier description of the fallen angels "in wandring mazes lost" of
"Vain wisdom all, and false Philosophie" [II, 561-
565]. Adam's arguments draw him by the same tor-
tuous motion to the abyss of despair:

> . . . all my evasions vain
> And reasonings, though through Mazes, lead me still
> But to my own conviction . . .   [X, 829-831]

Adam, whose reason was to be man's "guide," is lost
in tangles recalling the serpent's "mazie foulds" [IX,
161], from which Eve finally leads him by her special
powers which, since the earliest scenes in Eden, have
been differentiated from Adam's philosophical gifts.
In the first description of her "sweet attractive Grace"
[IV, 298]—more mellifluous, pictorial, and figurative
than the introduction of Adam; in her speeches before
the Fall, more lyrical, sensuous, and descriptive than
his; in the emphasis on her own loveliness and her

responsiveness to beauty first in her reflected "image" and then in the flowers to which she is often compared; in her susceptibility to "touch" and to dreams, Milton has defined her nature by special powers of feeling and imagination. Both Adam and Eve were created with the gift of eloquence, but hers is the "more simple, sensuous, and passionate" eloquence associated particularly with poetry.[10] Because grace moves fallen man through language that reaches his feelings and his imagination, because these are the qualities especially associated with Eve and expressed in her style, it is she through whom God works man's restoration.

In the human drama of *Paradise Lost,* Eve embodies the powers which are more largely represented by the poet who narrates it and his poem. His is the voice, innumerable illustrations have shown, which explicitly guides the reader through the complexities of his story, as Eve guides Adam away from the "Abyss" of despair. His poem—including within it the drama of Fall and recovery—is the vision which redeems our understanding of God's ways to men, as Eve's speech restores Adam's recognition of man's place in the Book of God's creatures, and therefore restores his ability to "rightly" name her as part of himself and as "Mother of Mankind" [XI, 159]. The nature of the poet's style is itself, then, an expression of his meaning, and for this reason, as we have seen, we are continually made to notice his *manner* of writing, by explicit assertions of its uniqueness[11] and by comparisons with other literary modes through imitation, allusion, and parody. His poem becomes the focus of our attention. It is offered as a more inclusive representation of the eloquence that Eve commands, the special language of poetry through which God moves fallen man.

It is this gift of eloquence for which the narrator of *Paradise Lost* prays in the opening passage when he invokes God's power to raise his fallen faculties:

> And chiefly Thou O Spirit, that dost prefer
> Before all Temples th' upright heart and pure,
> Instruct me, for Thou know'st; Thou from the first
> Wast present, and with mighty wings outspread
> Dove-like satst brooding on the vast Abyss
> And mad'st it pregnant: What in me is dark
> Illumine, what is low raise and support;
> That to the highth of this great Argument
> I may assert Eternal Providence,
> And justifie the wayes of God to men.   [I, 17-26]

The form of this prayer shows the poet's understanding—lost to man until Eve's speech restores it—of the divine origin of language, for the power that he invokes to purify his utterance is the Word that articulated order out of the chaos of the Abyss [III, 9-12; VII, 232-236]. His poetic intentions, as they are here defined, accord with the theory of language sanctioned by God, expounded by Abdiel, and shown to be true in the experience of unfallen man. These literary intentions are therefore to be seen in contrast to Satanic rhetoric, as the poet's epic manner is contrasted with Satan's "Vaunting" heroic style. The poet's intention, as it is phrased in this first invocation, is to "assert Eternal Providence," which is to use words for their original function of glorification rather than, as Satan arbitrarily imposes them, to "assert" his own will. The speaker's wish to "justifie the wayes of God to men" is not to abuse language in Satan's manner for self-interested persuasion, but like Eve to restore in man's darkened understanding true recognition of his relation to his Creator. The power to fulfill these intentions, the poet claims in the invocation to Book IX, is granted him by the spirit that "inspires/ Easie my unpremeditated Verse" [IX, 23-24], the grace which prompts the "unmeditated" eloquence of unfallen Adam and Eve. The "great Argument" to which his gift is dedicated is, like Eve's, the reconciliation of man to himself and God. The means for achieving this reconciliation is the special language of poetry. The true poem, then, performs the redemptive role in history that Eve's speech plays in the first human drama of sin and restoration. The true human author is the instrument of poetic eloquence which is the fullest expression of grace in the fallen world.

Absalom and Achitophel, like *Paradise Lost,* ends with a vision of order "Restor'd" in human history by divine intervention. The instrument of grace in the world of the satire is proclaimed to be the King's speech which, like Eve's words of reconciliation, marks the recovery following the temptation and fall:

> Thus from his Royal Throne by Heav'n inspir'd,
> The God-like *David* spoke: with awfull fear
> His Train their Maker in their Master hear.
>
> [936-938]

The echoes of the divine Maker's voice are audible in the King's tone as he assumes authority "like Heaven" [1000] to dispense justice as well as mercy, in the assurance of his predictions that right and law will prevail, and in the Biblical formula of his *fiats:* "Law they require, let Law then shew her Face" [1006]. The speech in part imitates the voice of the Creator establishing order out of chaos. At David's words the world is to be born anew, because they are divinely inspired words, and divinely approved:

> He said. Th' Almighty, nodding, gave Consent;
> And Peals of Thunder shook the Firmament.
>   [1026-1027]

This image of the Deity shaking the fabric of the heavens as confirmation of a promise is a traditional epic device,[12] but the lines point more specifically to *Paradise Lost* because of the echoes of Genesis in the preceding passage, the Biblical designation here of God as "Almighty," and especially because we have been so elaborately prepared from the beginning of the satire to notice the parallels between *Absalom and Achitophel* and Milton's archetypal story. David's proclamation of "Lawfull Pow'r" to be re-established in England is marked by the same divine confirmation as God's own promise in *Paradise Lost* to create the world and man [II, 351-353]. It is said to have almost the physical shaping force, the ruling power that Milton's Uriel ascribes to the divine Word in his account of the Creation:

> I saw when at his Word the formless Mass,
> This worlds material mould, came to a heap:
> Confusion heard his voice, and wilde uproar
> Stood rul'd, stood vast infinitude confin'd;
> Till at his second bidding darkness fled,
> Light shon, and order from disorder sprung . . .
>   [III, 708-713]

The simple certitude of the Biblical and epic formula, "He said," following David's speech, points to a chain of direct cause and effect: the King's inspired words

themselves have redemptive power when he utters them
from the throne. They are therefore intended to perform the function of Eve's reconciliation speech; they
are presented as the cause of order restored. The claim
in the poem is that David speaks a specially sacred language which brings a new golden age by restoring the
fallen world "Once more" to the ordered state in which
it was originally created:

> Henceforth a Series of new time began,
> The mighty Years in long Procession ran:
> Once more the Godlike *David* was Restor'd,
> And willing Nations knew their Lawfull Lord.
> [1028-1031]

This final vision of history redeemed, echoing Virgil's
Fourth or Messianic Eclogue, seems to complete the
analogy with *Paradise Lost,* giving Miltonic as well
as Virgilian pastoral associations to the political term
"Restor'd." But, as we have seen, at the same time
that Dryden elaborately establishes that analogy between his satire and Milton's epic, in the earlier parts
of the poem he cautions the reader not to respond to
the comparisons or parallels uncritically. From the
opening lines he warns us that some of our associations for Miltonic language are false, that the Biblical
and pastoral notions of an ideal state of nature out of
which Milton created his image of unfallen innocence
can be dangerously misleading. Throughout Dryden's
poem these traditional notions are attacked; repeatedly
the satire denies that the chaos of the modern world is
a corruption of an original state of innocence and harmony. *Absalom and Achitophel* pictures the origins of
history, rather, in the savage condition of nature unconfined, like Eden as Milton imagines it after the Fall,

and therefore denies the possibility of an ideal world to which by God's intervention the power of language can restore us. Nor is language itself represented, other than in the claims for David's speech, as a creation of God, or as the instrument of grace. Nowhere except in those lines framing the King's proclamation is there any suggestion that words have divinely sanctioned meanings which they were made to define. At no point in the satire are the characters made to speak in a language like the unfallen speech of Milton's Adam and Eve, directly reflecting the original conformity between man's understanding and the moral and theological meanings of God's creation. Even in the "pious times" of David's reign, with which in Dryden's opening passage the corrupt present seems at first to be contrasted, language is a kind of political makeshift at the mercy of interest and power. In fact, as we have seen, the only distinction made between language in its first form and in "modern" use is that it was originally less complicated: there were simply fewer words for human behavior, which is itself eternally the same. Words have, then, in Dryden's satire, no divine origins to which David's eloquence might return. They are not created by God to glorify His works in their first order and excellence, but invented by men, as "Priest-craft" invented the designation "sin," to serve factionalism and wield influence among the expediencies of human society. The assertions of divine power for the King's inspired utterance are therefore not rooted in attitudes toward language expressed earlier in the satire, are indeed contradicted by those attitudes. Having encouraged our scepticism about traditional literary associations, Dryden here fails when he attempts to exploit them as a means of asserting the unquestionable rightness of the King's position. Nor do the claims for sanctity seem descriptive of David's style, which mixes solemn echoes of Genesis with a casual profanity and ironic verbal play imitative of upperclass speech in a worldly society:

> Good Heav'ns, how Faction can a Patriot Paint!
> My Rebel ever proves my Peoples Saint ...
> [973-974]

We do not therefore hear in David's utterance what the lines framing it declare to be a miraculously powerful language, purified by grace of the abuses that characterize human speech elsewhere in the poem. It does not have the rightness of dramatic effect that we recognize in Eve's speech of reconciliation. The King not only uses words in ways resembling the style of other characters but holds the same attitude toward language. Rather shockingly, indeed, he acknowledges that, like Achitophel, he intends to triumph by manipulating the "arts" of language: he too will exploit as the instrument of his own political power the chaotic upheaval of words severed from meanings that is most fiercely exemplified in the poem by the Plot, here pictured in an allegorical form resembling Spenser's Errour and Milton's Sin:

> By their own arts 'tis Righteously decreed,
> Those dire Artificers of Death shall bleed.
> Against themselves their Witnesses will Swear,
> Till Viper-like their Mother Plot they tear:
> And suck for Nutriment that bloody gore
> Which was their Principle of Life before.
> [1010-1015]

Only the adjective "Righteously" distinguishes the King's exploitation of language from Achitophel's. Yet words like "Righteously," the satire has elsewhere taught us, can be appropriated by any opinion to describe any act or motive. Such terms are the tools of factionalism, which become effective only as power enforces their meaning. Indeed the King's predicted triumph, it can be seen in his own terms, is actually the simple triumph of "Pow'r" which will prove itself "Lawfull" by the event of victory:

> Their *Belial* with their *Belzebub* will fight;
> Thus on my Foes, my Foes shall do me Right:
> Nor doubt th' event: for Factious crowds engage
> In their first Onset, all their Brutal Rage;
> Then, let 'em take an unresisted Course,
> Retire and Traverse, and Delude their Force:
> But when they stand all Breathless, urge the fight,
> And rise upon 'em with redoubled might:
> For Lawfull Pow'r is still Superiour found,
> When long driven back, at length it stands
>   the ground.   [1016-1025]

The grounds of his moral authority are virtually those which Milton's Satan attributes to God: "Who now is Sovran can dispose and bid/ What shall be right . . . " [I, 246-247].

Although Dryden apparently intends that we should believe in the redemptive power of David's speech, we are not convinced by it as we are by Eve's appeal. For the monarch's claims seem finally to depend, not on the creative efficacy of eloquence restored, but on the arbitrary use of moral terminology to describe political aims, the cynical manipulation of verbal "arts" associated throughout the satire with the lawlessness of Achitophel's party. What the King would describe as "groundless Clamours" [995] if uttered by "Patriots" is for his own interest "Righteously decreed." What they call "Law" he names rebellion; what he calls "Lawfull" and "Superiour" is synonymous with effective "Pow'r." The style of the royal proclamation, to the modern reader unmoved by the political sympathies to which Dryden appeals,[13] therefore offers no satisfying alternative to the amoral abuses of language that elsewhere in his satire Dryden uses to characterize viciousness. The speech itself, for all its confident tone, does not represent a purified language with power to restore order to the chaos of human history.

Yet the narrator, the poet, claims that order *will* be restored, in lines which characteristically relate his prediction to the prophecies of other poets, and his final assertion bears more weight with the reader than the King's *fiats:*

> Henceforth a Series of new time began,
> The mighty Years in long Procession ran:
> Once more the Godlike *David* was Restor'd,
> And willing Nations knew their Lawfull Lord.
> [1028-1031]

When the poet declares what is "Lawfull" we tend to accept his assertion, not because we have forgotten his lessons about the shifting nature of such moral terms, not because we hear him use a newly purified language which returns to some belief (similar to Milton's theory) in the original and divinely sanctioned meanings for which words were created. We are inclined to accept the poet's claims, in ways that David's speech fails to convince, because we have learned in the course of the satire to trust him as a guide through the confusions of history.

Our confidence in the poet who interprets the action of *Absalom and Achitophel* depends upon qualities of his language which offer a contrast to the verbal abuses he depicts in the "modern" world. As in Milton's epic, and often by similar devices, we have seen, our attention is directed to the poet's style in order to underline such contrasts. Most obvious, perhaps, is the poet's capacity for ironic uses of words to allow a multiplicity of meanings. This ironic manner reveals his talent for holding more than one attitude at once, an ability dependent on his perception of the discrepancies or contradictions inherent in experience. We are aware of this kind of perception from the brilliant first couplet of the satire:

> In pious times, e'r Priest-craft did begin,
> Before *Polygamy* was made a sin ...

These lines force the reader to acknowledge at once several meanings for the word "pious." Most simply it means "Biblical or "patriarchal," but the speaker also equates it with the opposite of institutional religion and especially with ignorance of later moral terminology. To be "pious" means to act as impiously as people do now but to use a different vocabulary for such behavior, a definition that easily shades into the debased modern assumption that to be "pious" is to be shallowly, ostentatiously, or even hypocritically religious.[14] These meanings stand in uncriticized confusion side by side, none cancelling the others. The effect of such irony is of course first to amuse. It is characteristic of the poet that his view of the world allows him to appreciate its comic qualities and to make jokes about them that we are assumed to be capable of enjoying. This ironic exposure of discrepancies and contradictions inherent in experience, as it is designed to entertain, is also designed, even by its witty indirection, to insist upon the possibility of multiple interpretations of that experience. It demonstrates the absurdity of taking a narrow view: to do so would be to imitate the "pious Hate" [593] of a Shimei. Above all, it urges the need for sophisticated awareness, attested by the poet's own verbal agility, of the dangerous power of language which can disguise the nature of moral actions by giving them new or flattering names, as the poet himself wittily manipulates the reader's attitudes by inventing indulgent names for the King's promiscuity.

Combined with these evidences of his attitude are other habits of language which contrast the poet's style with the vicious rhetoric he condemns in the satire, and which therefore contribute to our sense of him as a trustworthy interpreter of the historical scene. There is an assurance displayed in his habitual repetition of generalizing phrases: "Two names, that always cheat and always please" [748] or "Still the same baite, and circumvented still" [754]. This kind of assurance is also implied by the characteristic use of rhetorical questions, which no speaker dares risk unless he has sufficient knowledge or command of his audience to predict their inevitable answer. Such confidence is born of a large view of events and people, an ability to place them in categories of experience which are applicable to the recurring patterns of individual behavior and of national history. This assurance is further guaranteed by another quality of response apparent in the poet's style, a quality which may be called *control*. We hear it most obviously in the

containment of his couplets, which give point and emphasis to each successive statement, tending to exclude
cadences suggestive of hesitation or a bewilderment of
feeling. Balance is the characteristic rhythmical pattern of this style:

> Oh foolish *Israel*! never warn'd by ill,
> Still the same baite, and circumvented still!
>
> [753-754]

Even in such exclamatory lines, the cadence is measured, suggesting the poet's habitual control over his
feelings and his fantasy, an exemplary contrast to the
hysterical clamor of the "Common Cry," as the dis-
interestedness implied by his balanced speech distinguishes the satirist from "all th' Haranguers of the
Throng,/ That thought to get Preferment by the
Tongue" [509-510].

These qualities of response revealed in his style
make the poet in *Absalom and Achitophel* a credible
interpreter to the reader of the chaotic world of human
history, so that our feelings can assent to his final
affirmation of order "Restor'd" in the closing lines
of the satire while we fail to be convinced by the logic
or style of the King's proclamation or the claims for
its divine sanction. It is the poet, rather than the
monarch, who embodies the means of recovery from
the disorders of society because it is he alone whose
voice represents an alternative to the abuses of
"modern" speech. The restorative power of language
is expressed in the poet's style—not because it is a
divinely inspired instrument of grace, not because it
re-establishes a belief in the necessary connection
between words and their moral or theological meanings, but because it is the controlled, assured, knowing

voice of experience, including the accumulated experience of literary tradition woven into his language by imitation, allusion, and parody. The poet's style offers an alternative to the "Impious Arts" [498] or "Cant" [521] of political leaders or the clamor of the herd "Who think too little, and who talk too much" [534], because it expresses the inclusive view which lifts him above faction and "meer instinct" [535]. His familiarity with the timeless world of literary tradition, enriching his observations of the immediate social scene in which he himself lives, endows him with the power of eloquence to restore "our byast Nature" —not to grace but to sanity.

In *Absalom and Achitophel,* then, the poet occupies a role comparable to that of the inspired bard in *Paradise Lost:* his eloquence, which is the special endowment of poetry, can rescue language from its debased use as an instrument of destruction in a corrupt society. Both works, therefore, claim the poet's function to be at once social and moral.

The bard of *Paradise Lost* does not present himself as a member of society in the sense that Dryden locates his satiric voice in time and place, by class and party. His style is deliberately stripped of purely local detail, conversational tones, social contexts. Yet the poet of Milton's epic is a man speaking "to men" out of "our" common experience in the fallen world, and his instrument, language, is consistently defined in the epic as a vehicle of "Social communication," "talk," "converse," between God and man, angels and man, man and wife.[15] The vision of the unfallen world which his poetic powers enable his fellow men to share is a vision of a universal community. Heaven itself in *Paradise Lost* resembles the "sweet Societies" where

Lycidas finds his final abode, a state where the angels gather together in "Festivals of joy and love/ Unanimous" [VI, 94-95] to eat and drink "in communion sweet" [V, 637]. Earth is created to share in this communion:

> . . . for God will deigne
> To visit oft the dwellings of just Men
> Delighted, and with frequent intercourse
> Thither will send his winged Messengers . . .
>   [VII, 569-572]

Four books of the poem demonstrate the original ease of such intercourse in the dialogue between Adam and the "sociable Spirit," Raphael [V, 221], sent by God to "Converse" with Adam "as friend with friend" [V, 229-230]—a phrase echoing Spenser's description of the "gladsome companee" of angels in the New Jerusalem.[16] The poet's ominous announcement of the Fall declares the end of this conversation between Heaven and Earth:

> No more of talk where God or Angel Guest
> With Man, as with his Friend, familiar us'd
> To sit indulgent, and with him partake
> Rural repast, permitting him the while
> Venial discourse unblam'd . . .   [IX, 1-5]

In the human drama, as we have seen, the consequences of sin are acted out as the loss of "sweet converse" from the time when Eve conceives of herself as "separate" [IX, 422, 424] to the moment when her eloquence restores her communion with Adam and theirs with God. The poet, celebrating that restoration, honors human conversation which is his definition of true marriage, and true marriage—the sanctified source of all "Relations dear" [IV, 756]—as his image of society. Fallen Adam and Eve take their "solitarie way" from Eden, but "hand in hand," [17] and the world they enter is the world of men, in which poetry is the means and expression of communion.

Dryden identifies his narrator as a social being in a more limited or specific sense, by his subject and his manner of speaking, yet the comparisons he makes in his poem with *Paradise Lost* (and the wealth of literary parallels included within that analogy) extend his social reference beyond the limits of his contemporary audience, the "we" of the *Essay of Dramatic Poesy.* By creating parallels which enable us to read *Absalom and Achitophel* as a local, modern instance of Milton's epic, he induces us to see in his image of Restoration society the moral workings of "our byast Nature" throughout human history. He insists—by imitation, allusion, parody, analogy—upon the interpretive power of his language, however social in the limited or particular sense, as a *poetic creation,* and on his shaping of the historical occasion as a *poem* in a living relationship to literary tradition. By these means he reiterates the claims of Milton for the role of the poet as a moral voice in the restoration of human society. And in so doing Dryden prepares the way for the achievements of Pope, whose poetry consistently shows "the follies of literature and of public and private life, by using a style that keeps alluding to values expressed and enshrined in the poetry of the Greco-Roman tradition. For Pope at the start of his career, as at the end, the imitation of life is also the imitation of literature." [18]

Part Two

SAMSON AGONISTES
and
ALL FOR LOVE

Dryden's uses of *Paradise Lost* in *Absalom and Achitophel* create connections between the epic and the satire as intricate and full of meaning as the literary relationship between any two works in English poetry. The richness of this relationship points to an extensive range of attitudes and feelings that Dryden could share with Milton, making such a comparison useful, therefore, as a corrective to our traditional separation of the two poets into sharply distinguished or alien worlds. This comparison also helps to unsettle our views of literary history in another way, by drawing attention to some important qualities of Dryden's writing which he learned in large part from his older contemporary, uses of language as central to his style as those which seem to distinguish him as a "new man" of letters representing the taste of a "modern" generation. This shift in emphasis— in no way denying the "line" of development traditionally traced in English literary history—allows us to place Milton's epic, as well as the satire so complexly dependent on it, firmly within the poetic tradition transmitted to Pope.

Dryden's sympathy with Milton's poetry was not limited to his assimilations from the epic, however. He was also familiar with *Samson Agonistes,* a work which the following chapter will argue to be altogether different in its fullest implications from *Paradise Lost.* In *All for Love,* I shall then try to demonstrate, Dryden showed the attraction—whether conscious or not—for him of precisely those qualities of style, those attitudes and feelings, which distinguish Milton's dramatic poem from his other work. The relationship between *All for Love* and *Samson Agonistes* is, we have said, of an altogether different kind from the connections traced between the satire and the epic. Because it does not seem to be a consciously articulated relationship, not a device deliberately contrived for the expression of meaning, it does not invite the same questions as those raised in previous chapters. Yet the large parallels as well as detailed resemblances we shall find between the two dramas seem to me illuminating because they are so numerous and because they include what is most distinctive, even peculiar, in each work. They suggest to me that *Samson Agonistes* made a strong impression upon Dryden whether or not he was aware of it as an influence shaping *All for Love,* that the impression was powerful because Dryden was largely sympathetic to the interpretation of experience in Milton's dramatic poem. The relationship between these two works therefore further complicates our reading of later seventeenth-century literary history. For they have in common qualities which reveal altogether different values from those honored in *Paradise Lost* and *Absalom and Achitophel. All for Love* and *Samson Agonistes* show Dryden and Milton to have shared also quite other sets of attitudes and feelings, which identify these poets with literary tradition in a different sense, as precursors of Romantic rather than Augustan poetry.

I

SAMSON'S "FORT OF SILENCE"

Milton's presentation of man's temptation, Fall, and redemption in *Paradise Lost* may be read as a legend of the morality of language. In this view, corrupt speech is the instrument of temptation; the fallen state is loss of eloquence; redemption is recovery of the creative powers of language, the restored communion of man with men and God. This rendering of the Biblical story places highest value upon articulation: it is the gift man shares with angels, likening him with them to their Creator, and it is the means of fulfilling his distinctively human nature as a creature designed for "sweet converse" with his fellow men. The poem expresses this evaluation by its dramatization of the story and the manner of its narration. The Fall and restoration of Adam and Eve, we have seen, is acted out in alterations of their style, and the redemptive role of eloquence is represented more largely in the poet whose vision includes their story, who explicitly directs our interpretation of it by calling attention to their modes of utterance and his own. His ways of guiding our responses to language, and therefore to the morality of his vision, are addressed to us as "men" aware of existing in a varied and inclusive context: the poet depends upon our shared familiarity with literature and all its traditional moral and social concerns. The poem is directed to us as we are heirs to that tradition and to the vast history envisioned in the epic, as we are members of the complex society which originates with the Fall of Adam and Eve.

Samson Agonistes, described in large terms, can be made to sound like a reworking of the attitudes expressed in *Paradise Lost.* Again Milton adapts an ancient literary form, this time Greek tragedy,[1] to the presentation of an Old Testament story, the fall and redemption of Samson, and again, we shall see, he shapes his material in the light of his attitudes toward language. Yet the reader at once recognizes the form and style of *Samson Agonistes* to be altogether different from *Paradise Lost,* with inevitably different implications. Here there is no narrator endowed by the creative gift of eloquence with authority to interpret the drama for the reader. Nor is the experience of the character dramatized in his own language in anything like the way in which the experience of Adam and Eve is revealed in their "alterd stile." Indeed, the most remarkable and puzzling quality of the poem is that it presents a hero whose development is never explained, nor is it acted out by the means Milton uses to present the human drama of *Paradise Lost.*

It is this quality which provoked Dr. Johnson's well-known assertion that the poem has a beginning and an end but "must be allowed to want a middle," [2] a complaint—like so many of his strictures on Milton's poems—productive of critical discussion continuing to our own time. In answer to Johnson, critics more favorable to the poem have usually claimed either that its central act is the intervention of grace working upon the inward man with a motion that is sudden and uncaused and which therefore ought not to be dramatized; or they have argued that the action of the poem is a dramatic sequence of temptations overcome within the hero's soul. The first answer, while theologically accurate, does not offer a full explanation of how the poem works. The second, if it be true, seems to me too broad a description to account in detail for the special uses of language which are so emphatic, so consistent, so elaborately patterned in *Samson Agonistes,* and which distinguish its style so markedly from Milton's epic verse. Neither line of argument about the structure and meaning of the poem has directed close attention to the precise groups of images used, we shall find, to express Samson's inward experience, nor explored in detail the remarkable, even peculiar, attitudes implied by Milton's choice of such imagery, his creation of this style.

The work opens with Samson lamenting his fallen state, from which by the end of the poem he is mysteriously redeemed. We understand that it is divine grace which brings about his restoration, as we are reminded in *Paradise Lost,* after the reconciliation scene, of "Prevenient Grace descending" to move fallen man toward his salvation. In the epic, Milton first provides an explanation of this motion when God reveals to Christ his plan for the redemption of fallen man, then dramatizes man's movement towards recovery in the domestic dialogues of Adam and Eve, and afterwards allows the narrator to repeat the theological argument for its divine cause. In *Samson*

Agonistes, however, the shift in direction is marked only by the hero's inscrutable announcement of "rouzing motions" within him, instantaneously effecting a change which disposes his destiny. The emphasis is upon the sudden, mysterious, inexplicable quality of his restoration: what happens to Samson is a miracle which escapes demonstration or explanation.

This rendering of the story from Judges xiii-xvi implies, then, an altogether different attitude toward language than Milton expressed in *Paradise Lost.* For if Samson's experience is felt to be inexplicable, then highest value in the poem is not placed upon articulation, but upon unutterable truths, inexpressible meanings. For this presentation of Samson's story, Milton therefore needed to create a form and style radically different from *Paradise Lost,* which would be directed to the reader in an altogether different manner from the richly allusive poetic language of his epic.

Samson Agonistes differs most obviously from *Paradise Lost,* and indeed all of Milton's other poetry, because it is a "Dramatic Poem," written in play form like the early *Comus* and unfinished *Arcades,* but unlike those aristocratic entertainments, according to Milton's preface never intended for performance. The choice of dramatic form may have been dictated in part by the Renaissance notion (still a compelling ideal for Milton and Dryden) that a great poet should contribute in both the major genres, epic and tragedy; but the peculiar qualities of language in *Samson Agonistes* imply other internal and expressive reasons for the choice of dramatic form as well as for the decision to write a play for reading rather than performance.[3]

A play differs from a narrative most simply because it does not demand a narrator, someone who knows the story and can tell it to the reader. A play can therefore seem more immediate. No speaker intervenes between the dramatized material and the audience to shape their interpretation: they must respond to it directly, without the modifying influence of a narrator's identity and opinions. A play which is read rather than performed can be in this sense even more intimate, for it dispenses with the actors who inevitably interpret the lines by their performance. Furthermore, a reader is an audience of one, whose solitary responses can be made to seem therefore more private, more inward, more individual, for he is free not only of such relationships as would inevitably be defined by a narrator's way of addressing him; he is also not a member of an audience of other men with whom he must stand in some sort of association. The form of a play to be read rather than acted is therefore particularly suited to the purposes of a writer who wishes to address the solitary reader as a private being, stripped in so far as possible of his worldly or social identity.

Milton's use of the form for this purpose is implied by his radical manipulations of it in *Samson Agonistes*. A dramatic poem differs from other literary types because it can avoid the presence of a speaker inevitable in narrative and lyric poetry, and at the same time exclude the visual effects inescapable in a drama that is performed.[4] For however simple the spectacle on a stage, the members of the audience see something, see at least the bodies of the actors, look at physical forms other than their own, contained by outlines, bearing weight, occupying space. In any dramatic performance the audience must inevitably see something outside themselves; this is one of the unique advantages of the theatre, and yet it is precisely this effect which Milton, writing a dramatic poem involving neither public performance nor spectacle, seemingly chose to avoid.

The opening lines of *Samson Agonistes* begin to explain Milton's use of dramatic form which yet avoids, it would appear deliberately, the visual effects that a play performed must inevitably have:

> *Sams.* A little onward lend thy guiding hand
> To these dark steps, a little further on;
> For yonder bank hath choice of Sun or shade,
> There am I wont to sit, when any chance
> Relieves me from my task of servile toyl,
> Daily in the common Prison else enjoyn'd me,
> Where I a Prisoner chain'd, scarce freely draw
> The air imprison'd also, close and damp,
> Unwholsom draught: but here I feel amends,
> The breath of Heav'n fresh-blowing, pure and sweet,
> With day-spring born; here leave me to respire.
> This day a solemn Feast the people hold
> To *Dagon* thir Sea-Idol, and forbid
> Laborious works, unwillingly this rest
> Thir Superstition yields me; hence with leave
> Retiring from the popular noise, I seek
> This unfrequented place to find some ease,
> Ease to the body some, none to the mind
> From restless thoughts, that like a deadly swarm
> Of Hornets arm'd, no sooner found alone,
> But rush upon me thronging, and present
> Times past, what once I was, and what am now.
>
> [1-22]

What is immediately surprising about these lines as the opening of a play intended to be read, not performed, is that they make virtually no effort to compensate to the reader for the visual effects that would be supplied automatically by performance, to an audience watching in a theatre. In fact, Milton seems deliberately to avoid these effects, as we can see by comparing his opening lines with Dryden's adaptation of them in the play *Œdipus* (written with Nathaniel Lee and performed in 1678).[5] The exchange of speeches in Dryden's version comes shortly after the stage direction, *"Enter* Tiresias, *leaning on a staff, and led by his daughter* Manto"*:

> *Tir.* A little farther; yet a little farther,
> Thou wretched daughter of a dark old man,
> Conduct my weary steps: And thou, who seest
> For me and for thyself, beware thou tred not,
> With impious steps, upon dead corps. Now stay;
> Methinks I draw more open, vital air.
> Where are we?
>
> *Man.* Under covert of a wall;
> The most frequented once, and noisy part
> Of Thebes; now midnight silence reigns even here,
> And grass untrodden springs beneath our feet.
>
> *Tir.* If there be nigh this place a sunny bank,
> There let me rest a while:—A sunny bank!
> Alas! how can it be, where no sun shines,
> But a dim winking taper in the skies,
> That nods, and scarce holds up his drowsy head,
> To glimmer through the damps? [I, i, pp. 144-145]

We know that Milton's opening lines are spoken by Samson because the stage directions name him and because, from our knowledge of the Biblical story, we are expected to identify him in his allusions to imprisonment by Dagon's worshippers. But we are never told who Samson is addressing, as Dryden identifies

Tiresias' guide, nor given any encouragement what-
soever to visualize his listener. No attendant is mentioned in the Argument to the poem, nor in the cast
of characters printed below it; there are no stage directions concerning such an attendant; and, most important, there are no suggestions in Samson's own
language to identify his listener as Tiresias' address
identifies Manto. The phrase "thy guiding hand" reveals that Samson is talking *to* someone, but because
those words are a traditional Biblical metaphor for
divine guidance, they might almost indicate that Samson is alone, speaking to God. We are only prevented
from thinking this because we recognize that he is
talking about immediate physical guidance, so that
the "guiding hand" must belong to someone walking
with him. Yet because we never *see* this person, we do
not even know when he ceases to be present. We only
learn that he has gone in line 20, when Samson speaks
of being "alone." The phrase "thy guiding hand"
therefore conveys a sense of Samson's ways of apprehending by physical touch, without inviting the
reader to visualize who is touching him.

The absence of visual detail in Milton's treatment
of the silent attendant also characterizes his presentation of the setting. He seems again deliberately to
avoid uses of language at the beginning of the poem
which would encourage the reader to imagine a scene
such as might be represented in a stage performance,
whereas Dryden's language sketches the setting by the
Theban wall in some detail, even though the theatre
audience is looking at the scene while the actors
describe it. Milton's stage directions indicate only that
the action takes place *"before the Prison in* Gaza,"
and again Samson's own language gives the reader
virtually nothing to look at (where Tiresias' description of the dim light is even unsuitably visual). He

indicates in line three that a certain "bank" is nearby, but he says nothing of its size, color, shape, material, texture, or location (except the indefinite "yonder"), says only that it offers him a "choice of Sun or shade." Because these are nouns (their effect is altogether different from Tiresias' descriptive adjective "sunny") and because they are not modified by any other words —as for example in such phrases as "brown shade" or "shade of the tree"—they are almost abstractions rather than images: they evoke no pictures. Again they teach the reader only so much about the setting as Samson himself can apprehend, through his sense of touch. He cannot *see* what "yonder bank" looks like, but he can *feel* the breezes "fresh-blowing, pure and sweet" and this feeling is what tells him, and the reader to whom his words communicate the sensation, that he is no longer inside the prison.

The opening of *Samson Agonistes* seems deliberately to prevent the reader from visualizing what would be presented on the stage by performance: Samson's attendant, his surroundings, and what is perhaps more important and more curious, Samson himself. The stage directions do not describe him. And in making the first one hundred and fourteen lines a soliloquy by Samson, a device entirely foreign to classical Greek tragedies,[6] Milton deliberately excludes the presence of another character who could describe the protagonist for the reader. We hear his voice. We can sense the rhythm of his movements—for example, by the pattern of pauses in the first two lines:

> A little onward lend thy guiding hand
> To these dark steps, a little further on . . .

We are invited to respond to his sensations of touch, especially by such adjectives as "close and damp," "fresh," "pure and sweet." Yet it would seem that we are, in so far as possible, prevented in the opening section of the poem from visualizing him as a figure in front of us, the way we would inevitably see him if his part were spoken by an actor in a stage perform- ance. That is, the reader is from the first discouraged from making the sorts of primary observations about Samson that we habitually make about people other than ourselves. As we hear him soliloquize, we do not observe with any distinctness the form or outline of his body, or the occupation of space that surrounds the body, or the relation of his body to other objects in space. We are not made at the beginning of the drama to look at him as a physical entity external to our- selves. Instead we are encouraged to feel with him: the impressions we receive from Samson's language in the soliloquy are for the most part versions of the sensations he himself receives, through hearing or touch or his own movements. For example, we do not learn about Samson's progress from the door of the prison to the bank on which he sits (or lies, or leans) by *seeing* him change his relation to objects in space, the way we would see an actor cross a stage, or the way Tiresias' words define his progress toward the wall. We learn that Samson has reached "yonder bank" only in a manner roughly parallel to the ways Samson himself learns it, by recording the different sensations caused upon the skin by "Sun," "shade," and "fresh" breezes.

The effect of this virtual absence of visual im- pressions in the beginning of the poem is to create a special relationship between the reader and the pro- tagonist. We are not only privileged to hear his words when he is speaking entirely to himself; we feel as if with his perceptions, almost as though we were inside his being. We are therefore in an association with him different from our social relationships, one more exclusively dependent, it would seem, upon elemental, almost visceral, sensations and primal feelings.

It is this peculiarly inward relationship which accounts for many of the strange effects in *Samson Agonistes*. Reading this play seems almost like listening to voices in the dark. The reader feels something like the same kind of straining, the same queer sensation of having his eyes open blankly to see nothing, the almost tactile awareness of sounds reaching his ears, and the suspicion that what is said has some weighted significance. Words seem to have a special character when they are uttered by a voice speaking out of the darkness surrounding a person we cannot see. The effect is again of a kind of abstraction or elevation from our usual social context, or perhaps a reaching inward to private feelings undistracted by it.

The reader's peculiar awareness of Samson is encouraged by the way in which his language characteristically calls attention to the presence of his body, usually not by making us visualize its shape, size, outline, or appearance, but by making us sense its physical properties and its enclosing limits. Reminders come in the frequent references to parts of the body which are obsessively named without being visually described—"eyes," "ears," "hair," "hand," "heart, head, brest, and reins" [609], "entrails, joints, and limbs" [614]. Equally numerous are references to the workings of Samson's body—"breath," "strength," "sleep," "feeling," "fainting," diseases, wounds and decrepitude—which can be felt but not seen. In addition to naming the parts and functions of his body, Samson habitually makes comparisons or contrasts between the body and the incorporeal self:

> O impotence of mind, in body strong!
> But what is strength without a double share
> Of wisdom, vast, unwieldy, burdensom . . .   [52-54]

In such passages he seems to distinguish physical from
spiritual being, yet since even to contrast them he
must speak of them in terms of each other, the contrast
is a reminder that his mind or soul exists within a body
which he cannot see but cannot escape from feeling.
This reminder is still more forcible when he uses language ordinarily referring to the body to form figures
of speech expressing his condition of spirit. An example is the extended simile (a type of figure seldom used
in the poem and therefore especially emphatic in its
rare occurrences) near the opening of his soliloquy:

> Retiring from the popular noise, I seek
> This unfrequented place to find some ease,
> Ease to the body some, none to the mind
> From restless thoughts, that like a deadly swarm
> Of Hornets arm'd, no sooner found alone,
> But rush upon me thronging, and present
> Times past, what once I was, and what am now.
>   [16-22]

Beginning with a contrast between mind and body, he
compares thoughts to insects that sting the flesh, a
simile which insists that the mind is encased in a physical form vulnerable to attack through its capacity for
feeling. Agony of the spirit is described as penetration
into the body, through "secret passage . . . To th' in-
most mind" [610-611], and the mind's workings are
more than once compared to insects attacking from
without:

Thoughts my Tormenters arm'd with deadly stings
Mangle my apprehensive tenderest parts,
Exasperate, exulcerate, and raise
Dire inflammation which no cooling herb
Or medcinal liquor can asswage,
Nor breath of Vernal Air from snowy *Alp*.

[623-628]

The definition of mental suffering is made in physical terms so violent and extreme that the tortured mind seems palpably enclosed in the mangled body.

These qualities of Samson's language are most fully illustrated in his descriptions of blindness:

The Sun to me is dark
And silent as the Moon,
When she deserts the night
Hid in her vacant interlunar cave.
Since light so necessary is to life,
And almost life it self if it be true
That light is in the Soul,
She all in every part; why was the sight
To such a tender ball as th' eye confin'd?
So obvious and so easie to be quench't,
And not as feeling through all parts diffus'd,
That she might look at will through every pore?
Then had I not been thus exil'd from light;
As in the land of darkness yet in light,
To live a life half dead, a living death,
And buried; but O yet more miserable!
My self, my Sepulcher, a moving Grave . . .

[86-102]

The remarkable beauty of the first four lines might re-call the blind bard's lament for lost sight in *Paradise*

Lost [III, 21-55], but that Samson's metaphors cause a feeling of strain by the odd force of the word "silent," which means literally "not shining" and retains its Latin meaning of "inactive," while also expressing the blind man's peculiar sense that ears see. The rest of the passage is entirely unlike the melancholy poetic lament of the epic narrator. Samson's loss of sight is characteristically described in raw physical terms: "quench't" used in connection with the "tender ball" of the eye. His experience is conceived in images of enclosure, confinement, imprisonment, in the queer figure of "feeling" peering out through the pores of the skin to the unseen world surrounding Samson, or more obviously in the metaphors of the blind body as a "Sepulcher" imprisoning him, or a "Grave." There is more painful physicality in these figures than in the image of the blind poet of *Paradise Lost* "In darkness, and with dangers compast round" [VII, 27]. The overpowering effect of Samson's metaphors, combined with the naming of parts and functions of the body and the violent comparisons of physical to spiritual experience, is to make the reader feel the enclosing limits of Samson's being almost as he does, as if from within, rather than observing them from without; for these are not visual images. His body does not *look* like a sepulcher or moving grave, but *feels* so to him.

Samson's habits of language create a pattern of contrasts between the imprisoned self, which is vulnerable to feeling, and the outside world, which is unseen and therefore threatening, alien, perhaps hostile. This contrast, established in the long opening soliloquy, is then acted out in the series of scenes which it introduces. Although the reader, who has been privileged to hear Samson's private recitation of feelings and in some sense to share them, experiences the action through his inward awareness of Samson, the other characters in the poem belong to the dark world surrounding him: they are locked out of the imprisoned self, as he is enclosed within it, and can only view him from without.

This pattern of contrasts shapes the introduction of the Chorus. Milton nowhere in the poem itself gives any description of the Chorus:[7] characteristically, we learn of their arrival as Samson does, only through hearing as he records the sounds first of their footsteps and then their voices:

> But who are these? for with joint pace I hear
> The tread of many feet stearing this way;
> Perhaps my enemies who come to stare
> At my affliction, and perhaps to insult,
> Thir daily practice to afflict me more.   [110-114]

The function of this question cannot be to keep the reader in suspense, since the Argument of the poem has already identified the characters in order of their arrival, the first visitors *"certain friends and equals of his tribe, which make the Chorus."* Its use is rather to emphasize Samson's separation from the unseen world of other human beings, whose threat to him is repeatedly associated in his imagination with the ability *to look at* his body while he, though imprisoned in darkness, is exposed, naked, made vulnerable by the capacity to receive sensations from without. Earlier he cursed himself "Made of my Enemies the scorn and gaze" [34], "dark in light expos'd" [75]; his return home is dreaded for fear he might become "to visitants a gaze,/ Or pitied object" [567-568]. Implied is a contrast between their *seeing* and blind Samson's *feeling,* which is enacted in the disposition of the first scene and repeated in those which follow it. The opening lines of the Chorus tell what they see when they look at Samson, the first visual description of any kind in the poem [118-123]. Those six lines, however, merely outline a figure in a traditional posture of despair, without filling in for the reader even as much individualized or pictorial detail as we are given by the narrator of *Paradise Lost* in his introductory description of Adam and Eve. The function of this brief passage, then, does not seem to be compensation for visual effects that would accompany stage performance. The language of the Chorus seems designed rather to make us aware that they apprehend through their eyes: "See how he lies . . ." [118], "Or do my eyes misrepresent?" [124]. Even in their imperatives to the blind hero they use inappropriately visual phrasing such as "But see . . ." [326] when Manoa enters, or at Harapha's appearance, "Look now for no inchanting voice" [1065]. This dependence of the Chorus on physical vision is further illustrated by their role as introducer of the other characters. At the opening of each succeeding episode, they provide Samson with a description of the entering figure, which places that person as well as themselves in the world of visual appearances from which the hero is cut off. This point is emphasized especially by their description of Dalila [710-724], the most elaborate, most nearly pictorial "view" [723] in the poem, which is an appropriate way to introduce the character who most fully represents the threats to Samson in the alien world of appearances.

Like the Chorus, the other characters introduced by them are presented as viewing Samson from outside, as the reader, with his inward awareness, does not. Milton's language constantly reminds the reader that these characters, in contrast to Samson himself, apprehend through their eyes. For example, Manoa's first words are, like the Chorus' a lament for the "miserable change" [340] in what he sees of Samson's appearance and surroundings; again the emphasis is upon Manoa's visual mode of apprehension. We are made aware in Manoa's exclamation that he is overcome by what his eyes behold, yet Milton does not design the character's words to paint a picture of Samson. In the next episode, when Dalila approaches, the Chorus tells Samson: "Yet on she moves, now stands & eies thee fixt" [726]. She herself offers as the first motive for her visit the desire "to behold/Once more thy face" [741-742], but again the figure of Samson upon which she gazes is not described to the reader. Then when Harapha arrives, he explicitly announces that his purpose is to learn what Samson looks like, to see if his appearance coincides with his heroic fame:

> And now am come to see of whom such noise
> Hath walk'd about, and each limb to survey,
> If thy appearance answer loud report. [1088-1090]

In the final episode, the messenger leads Samson off to be a public "spectacle" [1542, 1604] before the gaze of all his enemies. By presenting the Chorus and other characters, whether friendly or hostile, as observers of Samson's outward appearance, Milton emphasizes the contrast between the experience of the blind man encased within his dark body and the ways of men in the unseen world surrounding him. In these contrasting terms the Chorus themselves observe him, echoing Samson's own metaphors of confinement, imprisonment, enclosure—but with a difference:

> Which shall I first bewail,
> Thy Bondage or lost Sight,
> Prison within Prison
> Inseparably dark?

Thou art become (O worst imprisonment!)
The Dungeon of thy self; thy Soul
(Which Men enjoying sight oft without cause
   complain)
Imprison'd now indeed,
In real darkness of the body dwells,
Shut up from outward light
To incorporate with gloomy night . . .   [151-161]

Sympathetically, the Chorus imagine Samson imprisoned in the dungeon of his blind body, but they are
looking at it from outside. What they recognize is his
separateness, his inaccessibility: they cannot see into
what they call the "Inseparably dark" recesses of his
being.
   If eyesight cannot penetrate the blind man's inward experience, words are equally ineffectual. Language, as much as outward vision, is associated with
the alien world surrounding Samson, and this pattern
of contrasts is also acted out in his encounters with
the other characters. For instance, when the Chorus
first see him, they are reluctant to speak to him:

This, this is he; softly a while,
Let us not break in upon him . . .   [115-116]

The phrase "break in" suggests penetration by some
outer force. Here and throughout the poem words
spoken to him by others are like alien bodies, existing
outside the hero's private world. Repeatedly words are
imagined metaphorically as if they were *things*. After
the Chorus first speaks, Samson says:

I hear the sound of words, thir sense the air
Dissolves unjointed e're it reach my ear. [176-177]

"Dissolves unjointed," although it actually refers to "sense," seems to make the words themselves into physical objects, with weight, substance, texture, and a structure of movable parts. In the next speech the Chorus endows words with tangible properties by talking of them as medicinal salves or "Balm" [184-186]; Manoa also urges Samson to "admit" the "healing words" of his friends [605]; Dalila's "words addrest seems into tears dissolv'd" [729], or they seem to Samson as "false pretexts and varnish'd colours" [901] covering her guilt like the pieces of a costume or disguise. When he hears Manoa coming he exclaims:

> Ay me, another inward grief awak't,
> With mention of that name renews th' assault.
> [330-331]

Although here "grief" is the metaphorical weapon, its means of entry, as it were, is the sound of the "name" itself.

The association of language, words, speech with the unseen world threatening the hero imprisoned in his blindness is intensified by Samson's characteristic way of imagining his downfall as the surrender to Dalila's words as if they were physical weapons:

> She was not the prime cause, but I my self,
> Who vanquisht with a peal of words (O weakness!)
> Gave up my fort of silence to a Woman. [234-236]

Or her words are magical poison:[8]

> So much of Adders wisdom I have learn't
> To fence my ear against thy sorceries. [936-937]

This pattern of metaphors, imagining words as physical entities with which the characters attempt to penetrate the "Inseparably dark" recesses of Samson's being, works with the repeated figures of enclosure to point out the separation of the blind hero from other human beings. They can look at him, but what they see is only the enclosing outline, the outward appearance of his body. They can talk to him, but their speech is alien and ineffectual: their "talk" is as remote from his inward experience as is their physical vision of his body.

The contrast which is acted out in the scenes between Samson and the other characters—the contrast between their relation to the visible world outside themselves and the blind man's—is defined then by the difference in their relation to language, speech, and therefore to human society. This distinction is implied in Samson's very first words to the Chorus:

> Your coming, Friends, revives me, for I learn
> Now of my own experience, not by talk,
> How counterfeit a coin they are who friends
> Bear in their Superscription (of the most
> I would be understood) in prosperous days
> They swarm, but in adverse withdraw their head ...
>   [187-192]

These lines courteously acknowledge the presence of the Chorus (although they show distrust of the word "friends" as an empty name, associated with swarming insects and darting adders or serpents) but do not answer what they have said. It is their "coming," not their "apt words" [184], which revives Samson. Indeed, he seems deliberately to ignore their words. Speaking of himself, he contrasts what he has learned from his "own experience" with what can be learned from "talk," a word which by its curiously colloquial sound here implies a scornful tone—"mere talk." It is significant, however, that the form of talk he is derogating here is not idle chatter, malicious slander, or the betrayal of secrets, but abstract generalizations, or moral maxims. This talk is of the kind which the Chorus brings to Samson—"Counsel," "Consolation," "apt words" [183-184]. They value such words as solace, palliative, medicine; Samson dismisses them as irrelevant to "experience." Here then is another form of the contrast between the outside world and the inward self, the difference between abstract moral generalizations which can be apprehended by the intellect, and the truth of individual experience, which is felt. The most explicit statement of this contrast is made by the Chorus when they have heard Samson's despairing lament. Typically they echo with variations his images of the spirit suffering in a tortured and diseased body, from which they acknowledge their separation:

> Many are the sayings of the wise
> In antient and in modern books enroll'd;
> Extolling Patience as the truest fortitude;
> And to the bearing well of all calamities,
> All chances incident to mans frail life
> Consolatories writ
> With studied argument, and much perswasion
>   sought
> Lenient of grief and anxious thought,
> But with th' afflicted in his pangs thir sound
> Little prevails, or rather seems a tune,
> Harsh, and of dissonant mood from his complaint,
> Unless he feel within

> Some sourse of consolation from above;
> Secret refreshings, that repair his strength,
> And fainting spirits uphold.   [652-666]

Recognizing the abyss between the blind man and themselves, they imagine their own speeches to reach him as mere "sound" or as a jarringly frivolous "tune," and yet paradoxically their very statement of this separation emphasizes its inescapability since they phrase it in the sort of "talk" that Samson has already brushed aside as irrelevant, even painful to his feelings.

This paradox is at the heart of the Chorus' relation to Samson, indeed at the heart of the poem itself, as it must almost inevitably be in any work of literature which denies to language the power of expressing what the work itself implies to be the truth of experience. If in *Samson Agonistes* Milton defines speech as inadequate, if words are threatening to the hero, if language is irrelevant to feelings whose intensity and inescapability define the experience of his inward self, Milton must acknowledge his own verbal recreation of that experience to be inadequate. Or—and this is the alternative I believe he chose—he must create for it a poetry quite unlike the elaborately articulated, literary language of *Paradise Lost*. For the dramatic poem he must create a style which seems to reach for its effects beyond the realm of articulation and therefore expresses truths which, we shall see, seem to escape the limits of human language itself.

Some of the peculiarities of Milton's style in the dramatic poem appear as if designed to present the reader with an inward awareness of Samson's nature and experience independent of his outward appearance, upon which the other characters must depend for their vision of him. Other qualities of the style may be thought of as creating in the reader an awareness of Samson's inward being which also seems to be independent, in a very special sense, of the words which are spoken by him or about him by the other characters who talk to him.

To say that the reader's awareness of Samson is in some way independent of language is of course to speak metaphorically. As in any other poem, in a play written to be read, not performed, we literally have only its language (however richly that may refer to matters outside the work) by which to interpret it. Yet the effect in Milton's poem is that we come to know Samson by very special means. It is *as if* we do not learn to understand his experiences by the same means as we learn about Adam and Eve or Satan—by what he says about himself, or by words spoken to him, or words spoken about him; the effect is as if we come to know Samson by what is *not* said. There is a strange way in which, being discouraged from visualizing the protagonist and his surroundings, we apprehend him chiefly as a voice, which we strain to hear in the darkness, listening for the unspoken significance of his words, until finally we seem to hear even his silences.[9] These silences are of course ultimately the creation of Milton's language. They are endowed with significance by his shaping of dramatic form and style, by verbal means, but their effect is as if they reached us by means which are unarticulated, unspoken, wordless.

The opening lines of the poem begin our education in reading as if we were apprehending unsaid meanings, which surpass the reach of human utterance:

A little onward lend thy guiding hand
To these dark steps, a little further on;

> For yonder bank hath choice of Sun or shade,
> There am I wont to sit, when any chance
> Relieves me from my task of servile toyl,
> Daily in the common Prison else enjoyn'd me,
> Where I a Prisoner chain'd, scarce freely draw
> The air imprison'd also, close and damp,
> Unwholsom draught: but here I feel amends,
> The breath of Heav'n fresh-blowing, pure and
>   sweet,
> With day-spring born; here leave me to respire.
>   [1-11]

By line three the reader learns that Samson is talking to some unidentified attendant who is leading him towards a nearby bank where he will rest; but the very first line, we have said, hints at another meaning in the phrase "thy guiding hand," a traditional Biblical formula for divine inspiration.[10] This association is supported by other details of language. The repetition of the entreaty sounds like a prayer: "A little onward lend thy guiding hand/ To these dark steps, a little further on." The words "onward" and "further" repeated in a prayer form suggest some kind of spiritual progress toward a goal, which is defined as the traditional Christian reward of "rest." Adjectives like "dark," "servile," "Unwholesom," although they refer to such physical facts as "steps," "toyl," "air," have moral implications as well. These devices of language all prepare for the louder Biblical associations of Samson's reference to the breezes:

> . . . but here I feel amends,
> The breath of Heav'n fresh-blowing, pure and
>   sweet,
> With day-spring born . . .   [9-11]

The metaphor of the "breath of Heav'n" implies a living connection between God and his world, infusing such physical properties as purity and sweetness with moral or theological meanings and providing "amends," a word suggesting some kind of "repairing," "healing," "restoring" property which can be felt by a suffering human being. Finally, "day-spring" is an expression exclusively Biblical in its associations, a metaphor for the rising sun and the Son of God.

Milton's manipulation of dramatic form and language in these opening lines has, it can be seen, a double effect. The absence of visual detail describing characters or setting encourages the reader to apprehend by other means than sight, as Samson does, as if from within his being. Yet the uses of language just discussed create another effect, which might almost seem to contradict what we have defined as the reader's inward awareness of Samson. The Biblical allusions, the echo of prayer forms, the moral or theological connotations of the diction, even the rhythmical suggestion of progress toward a goal of rest, all work upòn the reader (who in addition is assumed to know the outcome of Samson's story) with the effect that the reader hears in the language what may be called, in a specially defined sense, its unspoken meanings. That is to say, Samson is talking about physical guidance, actual breezes, bodily rest, and the reader apprehends these physical experiences in a manner similar to Samson's own ways of feeling. At the same time, in the opening lines the reader also responds to other meanings for Samson's words, meanings of which even the hero, *in the beginning of the poem,* is unaware.[11] This implies that although we are entirely dependent upon Samson's language in order to apprehend his sensations and his relation to the unseen world around him, at the same time we hear in his words meanings which cannot be apprehended by the senses, which seem in some fashion to be unspoken.

To define the special effect of this language, one might set Samson's soliloquy beside Eve's in Book IX of *Paradise Lost,* uttered just after she has eaten the forbidden fruit. In lines 816 to 833, for example, she calculates her future behavior toward Adam:

> But to *Adam* in what sort
> Shall I appeer? shall I to him make known
> As yet my change, and give him to partake
> Full happiness with mee, or rather not,
> But keep the odds of Knowledge in my power
> Without Copartner? so to add what wants
> In Femal Sex, the more to draw his Love,
> And render me more equal, and perhaps,
> A thing not undesireable, somtime
> Superior; for inferior who is free?
> This may be well: but what if God have seen,
> And Death ensue? then I shall be no more,
> And *Adam* wedded to another *Eve,*
> Shall live with her enjoying, I extinct;
> A death to think. Confirm'd then I resolve,
> *Adam* shall share with me in bliss or woe:
> So dear I love him, that with him all deaths
> I could endure, without him live no life.

The contrast is revealing because certainly in Eve's speech, as in Samson's, the reader hears meanings of which the speaker is unaware. But they are of a different kind. Eve's language reveals unconscious confusions, the substitution of one feeling for another, the distortion of emotion, the development of conflicting attitudes. She can no longer distinguish, for instance, between exerting "power" and being "free"; she claims to "love" Adam while she expresses envy and resentment of him; she declares her intention to "share" as if generously, when her resolve is rather to possess. Her language therefore shows us more of her inner life than she herself can recognize, but it does not, like Samson's, refer to a whole order of meanings of whose existence she is unaware. Instead her words show that her responses to her experiences are not quite what she thinks they are. There are contrasts in her language between what it states and what it expresses, even contradictions between what she asserts about herself and what she reveals, and through these discrepancies Milton dramatizes for the reader the inward experience of the character. This manipulation of language is familiar to us in all sorts of literary works. What is said of Eve's soliloquy can in large terms apply to Hamlet's meditations, to the words of Donne's lovers, to Absalom's speeches; it is the artistic organization and concentration of language used in ways selected from the ways men actually speak in their daily lives.

Milton's language in the opening of *Samson Agonistes* works quite differently. Although the reader is aware of meanings other than those intended by Samson, the two kinds of meanings are not in contrast or conflict: what Samson states is not contradicted by what he expresses. The difference between the reader's view of the hero's experience *at the beginning of the poem* and Samson's own view is that we apprehend his experience as if with his feelings, from within, but at the same time we are also aware of another dimension to it. The reader recognizes the blind man's words as referring to another order of experience, which does not conflict with his spoken assertions;

there is no dramatic interplay between the two. The "guiding hand" to which he refers *is* the hand of his unseen companion, and it is also the leading spirit of divine grace guiding Samson unawares toward a final goal of rest for his tortured spirit. Both meanings are true, although only the reader *in the beginning* hears both. Samson's words apply to true facts of his immediate experience, but they also act for the reader almost as terms in a series of metaphors connecting these true facts to meanings which are unspoken but equally true. Blindness is for Samson, and for the reader with his inward awareness of the hero, the physical condition of being imprisoned in enclosing darkness, of depending on touch and hearing, in need of literal guidance, vulnerable to unseen attack. This is the experience to which Samson's words refer, but for the reader, who can even from the first lines interpret these words metaphorically, blindness also means a condition of the spirit, a state of freedom from distraction by the "various objects of delight" [71] in the visible world, a receptivity to guidance and a heightened responsiveness to inward "motions" and to the "breath of Heav'n." Because only one meaning is actually intended by Samson, who in the earlier parts of the poem applies his words literally rather than metaphorically, and because there is no dramatic connection between the two orders of significance, the reader's grasp of another meaning seems to be independent of the blind man's speech, to have its source elsewhere than in his words, and therefore in that sense to escape, as it were, the limits of human language.

In fact the reader's awareness of metaphorical significance in Samson's words depends on his knowledge of the Old Testament story and his familiarity with traditional Christian phraseology. Because we know that the poem will end with Samson's triumphant death as God's chosen champion, we can recognize the sense in which he is guided from above without his knowledge. Because we are familiar with the metaphorical use in Scripture of certain clusters of words[12] —such as "dark," "blind," "sight," "light," "guide," "rest," "bondage," "ransom," "free"—as Milton repeats these over and over in *Samson Agonistes* we recognize their metaphorical meanings even when those meanings are not intended or understood by the speaker who utters them.

Unlike the reader, the characters in the poem who are dependent on ordinary ways of knowing, by outward vision or through human "talk," do not hear metaphorical meanings in the language describing Samson's experience. This contrast is expressed in the first speech of the Chorus. To the Chorus Samson's blindness means only the "real darkness of the body" which they view from without:

Which shall I first bewail,
Thy Bondage or lost Sight,
Prison within Prison
Inseparably dark?
Thou art become (O worst imprisonment!)
The Dungeon of thy self; thy Soul
(Which Men enjoying sight oft without cause complain)
Imprison'd now indeed,
In real darkness of the body dwells,
Shut up from outward light ...   [151-160]

Their uses of the words "indeed" and "real" are most revealing. They are contrasting a metaphorical conception of the soul's imprisonment in the body with the fact of sightlessness as a physical bondage. It is the physical fact which is "real," for reality means to them whatever is literal, palpable, what can be apprehended in deed by the senses. Although their manner of speaking about Samson here shows that the Chorus respond with sympathy to what they see, as later they respond to the words he speaks, they do not recognize in his immediate experiences any other order of meanings. To them loss of "Sight" means a terrible physical mutilation; they do not also conceive of blindness as a groping and vulnerable condition of the spirit. To them Samson's "Bondage" means confinement in the prison or the chains or the body they can see; they are not simultaneously aware of it as an inward captivity, the imprisonment of the soul within its own lacerated feelings. They are unaware of the unspoken meanings for which the reader has been prepared to listen, from the very first lines of the poem, and such unawareness of metaphorical significance characterizes the responses of other figures in their confrontations of Samson. When the blind man finally agrees to perform for the Philistines, for example, the Officer says:

> I praise thy resolution, doff these links:
> By this compliance thou wilt win the Lords
> To favour, and perhaps to set thee free.
>
> [1410-1412]

Because he depends on what he hears and sees, the Officer accepts Samson's words as "compliance" and defines his freedom as release from chains and from the prison house. In contrast, the reader, who has other ways of apprehending, recognizes the unspoken significance of the chains, identifying them metaphorically with inward captivity, and freedom with a spiritual condition not dependent on the will of the Philistines. Or to take one more example, Manoa's final plan for Samson is to bring his body in heroic state "With silent obsequie and funeral train/ Home to his Fathers house" [1732-1733]. This triumphant return is identified metaphorically for the reader with the return of Samson's spirit to God, a significance which (in fact dependent on our knowledge of Biblical narrative and phraseology) is not intended by Manoa and seems to be expressed as if by means other than the human speech of the character in the poem whose actual words we hear.

The Old Testament story of Samson obviously attracted Milton for one reason, we have seen, because it was the story of a blind hero and therefore allowed the poet to explore the expressive possibilities of a blind man's peculiarly significant relationship to the visible world. In *Samson Agonistes* the visible world is identified with the society of men (the ideal, literary, pastoral world from which the blind bard of *Paradise Lost* feels himself to be cut off is excluded from concern in the dramatic poem). The society of men is represented by the characters who visit the blind man and they in turn are defined by their language. The choice of Samson as his hero therefore also allowed Milton to exploit the story of a man whose experience involves a peculiarly significant relationship to human speech.

This specially meaningful relationship to language depends in part on the fact of Samson's blindness itself. Not being able to see, he receives his knowledge of the world around him most often through other people's words, a circumstance which Milton repeatedly

calls to the reader's attention by innumerable references to "words," "sayings," "talk," "speech,"
"sounds," "tongues," "ears," "hearing," as well as
by the pattern of metaphors endowing words, we have
seen, with palpable, physical existence, as if they were
alien bodies that might actually penetrate the enclosing
limits of the hero's body.

Samson's story also enabled Milton to present
him in a peculiarly significant relationship to language
because he was a man entrusted by God with a secret,
who sinned by telling that secret.[13] Milton gives almost
as much emphasis, we shall find, to this aspect of
Samson's story as to his blindness, with effects as
richly expressive. He might have chosen rather to
present Samson's sin exclusively as a violation of his
vow of abstinence, a sexual lapse, a vicious susceptibility to touch, to feeling, to physical ease and delight.
Or he could have made Samson's lapse seem primarily
a kind of forgetfulness or triviality, or a failure to
act, or prideful self-assertiveness. The opportunities
for emphasis are innumerable, and although the language in its most remarkable and most consistent
patterns seems to point to a different and more special
reading of the story, Milton in fact suggests some-
where in the poem most of these possibilities. Despite
Samson's claims to divine guidance in his choice of
wives, for example, the Chorus seem to share Manoa's
interpretation of the Nazarite's sin as his marriage to
an unclean Philistine "Against his vow of strictest
purity" [319, 420], Milton's decision to make Dalila
Samson's wife rather than concubine preventing his
sin from being defined as fornication. Elsewhere the
Chorus sympathize with him as a figure illustrating
the maxim that "wisest Men/ Have err'd, and by bad
Women been deceiv'd" [210-211], a palliative interpretation of his fault later swept aside by Samson with

bitterest self-mockery [381-401]. Dismissing the excuse of ignorance, Samson himself blames his downfall on unwariness nurtured by vainglory and sensuality:

> Then swoll'n with pride into the snare I fell
> Of fair fallacious looks, venereal trains,
> Softn'd with pleasure and voluptuous life . . .
>
> [532-534]

Or he attributes the surrender of his manhood to his impious reliance upon stupid strength, "Proudly secure, yet liable to fall/ By weakest suttleties" [55-56]. Throughout the poem we are offered such explications of Samson's sin, some rejected by the hero himself, some supported by his own feelings, all contributing to the impression of the enormity of his sin. Within this context, however, the fullness of meaning seems to be concentrated in related patterns of language, in recurring groups of images—many of them discussed earlier in this chapter—which consistently represent Samson's fall as a violation of his proper relation to language.

Samson seems to offer such an interpretation of his sin when he first accuses himself early in his soliloquy:

> Whom have I to complain of but my self?
> Who this high gift of strength committed to me,
> In what part lodg'd, how easily bereft me,
> Under the Seal of silence could not keep,
> But weakly to a woman must reveal it,
> O'recome with importunity and tears.   [46-51]

The definition of his vow as a "Seal of silence" calls attention to its violation by the betrayal of God's secret rather than, for example, by intemperance; the surrender of his manhood is to the power of "importunity and tears" rather than to more specifically sexual seductions. Again with the same emphasis he speaks of his "folly, who have profan'd/ The mystery of God giv'n me under pledge" [377-378], using "profan'd" in its more general sense but also with its Latin meaning, to "disclose a secret." In his most elaborate explication of his fault he expands the same interpretation. To his father he argues:

> . . . let me here,
> As I deserve, pay on my punishment;
> And expiate, if possible, my crime,
> Shameful garrulity. To have reveal'd
> Secrets of men, the secrets of a friend,
> How hainous had the fact been, how deserving
> Contempt, and scorn of all, to be excluded
> All friendship, and avoided as a blab,
> The mark of fool set on his front?
> But I Gods counsel have not kept, his holy secret
> Presumptuously have publish'd, impiously,
> Weakly at least, and shamefully: A sin
> That Gentiles in thir Parables condemn
> To thir abyss and horrid pains confin'd. [488-501]

His impiety is verbal rather than sexual. Explicitly Samson defines his crime as "Shameful garrulity," shameful because it was the betrayal of a secret, above all a holy secret. But the passage is full of contempt so exaggerated that it almost seems to be contempt for speech itself: the loathing in the term "blab," for example, as if it were the worst, the most ignominious name he could be called, as if blabbing itself were the most repulsive of sins, as if all "garrulity" were shameful. With the same contempt he repeatedly names his sin as the betrayal of God's secret. He reminds Dalila how she exploited his love for her until he "unbosom'd all my secrets to thee,/ Not out of levity, but over-powr'd/ By thy request" [879-881]. When he dismisses her he recalls his "folly" in similar terms:

> So let her go, God sent her to debase me,
> And aggravate my folly who committed
> To such a viper his most sacred trust
> Of secresie, my safety, and my life.   [999-1002]

As Samson's sin is defined to be the giving away of a secret or violation of a "sacred trust of silence/ Deposited within" him [428-429], his temptation is repeatedly interpreted as the admission of hostile words. This is the remembrance which again evokes his self-contempt:

> How could I once look up, or heave the head,
> Who like a foolish Pilot have shipwrack't,
> My Vessel trusted to me from above,
> Gloriously rigg'd; and for a word, a tear,
> Fool, have divulg'd the secret gift of God
> To a deceitful Woman . . .   [197-202]

Dalila's weapons are not most characteristically represented to be the attractions of beauty or sexuality, the temptations of sight or touch, but rather—as in this passage—they are imagined to be powerful sounds. She is a temptress luring the Pilot from his course with seductions defined here by Samson and elsewhere by the Chorus in images associating her powers with the Sirens' "inchanting voice," the "bait of honied words" [1065-1066].[14] More often, numerous passages already quoted have shown, Samson defines her words as weapons which "O'recome" and break down his inner defenses:

> Yet the fourth time, when mustring all her wiles,
> With blandisht parlies, feminine assaults,
> Tongue-batteries, she surceas'd not day nor night
> To storm me over-watch't, and wearied out.
> At times when men seek most repose and rest,
> I yielded, and unlock'd her all my heart . . .
> [402-407]

The military language here and in similar passages [879-881, 906] suggests heroic struggle between mighty enemies, but more precisely the metaphor makes Dalila's words "storm" him as weapons bombard besieged ramparts. This meaning is supported by his definition of surrender as having "unlock'd" his heart, as if opening gates to an enemy. Dalila confesses her own motives in corresponding metaphors:

> No better way I saw then by importuning
> To learn thy secrets, get into my power
> Thy key of strength and safety . . .   [797-799]

The same pattern of imagery is repeated in another of Samson's self-accusations, where again he blames his fall on his susceptibility to the power of Dalila's words:

>   . . . of what now I suffer
> She was not the prime cause, but I my self,
> Who vanquisht with a peal of words (O weakness!)
> Gave up my fort of silence to a Woman.   [233-236]

Here he defines his vow figuratively as a "fort of silence," a metaphor recalling his very first reference to the "Seal of silence" [49] and drawing together many other uses of language in an inclusive interpretation of Samson's experience. The image of surrendering a beleagured "fort" defines at once the nature of his sin and the trust which he betrayed. Samson thinks of his sacred destiny as the command or defense of a fortress, an image related to descriptions of his present confinement in the prison of the Philistines and in his own blinded body. Like a prison, a fort is a physical enclosure, separating its inmate from a threatening world, locking him within a barrier which also keeps his enemies out. To command a fort is to use enclosure and separation for heroic defense. To unlock the gates can mean to desert the fort or to admit the enemy, allowing the captured fort to become a prison, in which enclosure and separation signify the inmate's servile submission. In this way, Dalila, by capturing the "key" to Samson's secret, intended to make him "Mine and Loves prisoner" [808]. To surrender a "fort of silence" means in Samson's own interpretation to betray his destiny by admitting hostile sounds and by uttering forbidden words, thus to violate his divinely ordained relationship to language.

Samson, then, is at the beginning of the poem particularly vulnerable to language because speech is virtually his only connection with the unseen world around him. Yet the words of the other characters, even spoken in sympathy or counsel, are imagined as alien bodies, or weapons used against him, while his own words are described as sins, crimes, disgrace, shame. Admitting words or speaking them is equated for Samson with weakness and vice; strength and virtue are associated with silence. His divinely appointed task as God's champion is expressed in images of heroic action—"The deeds themselves, though mute, spoke loud the dooer" [248]—but in Milton's presentation of Samson's story, heroic action is included in the metaphor for guarding the "fort of silence." [15]

The blind man himself rarely refers to his past deeds, dismissing such boasting as suited to a braggart like Harapha, whom he taunts as "Tongue-doubtie" [1181], a satirical epithet showing the hero's characteristic contempt for "talk." More often he uses the language of battle figuratively, as we have seen in his descriptions of his surrender to Dalila. Samson there represents his fall as a military failure but that martial language is used altogether metaphorically: the battle is verbal, the enemy's weapons are "Tongue-batteries," the hero's lapse is to have "unlock'd" his heart, admitting words and allowing them to escape. To regain his heroic stature he must restore the silence within himself which it was his divinely appointed task to guard. What this implies is that he must learn to prevent words from penetrating his being, and he must learn to give none away. Or, in Milton's most extreme images, what Samson must do to fulfill his heroic task is to become not only blind to the appearances of the visible world. He must become deaf to its spokesmen and finally mute. This progress Milton's manipulation of dramatic form and style reveals to the reader. It is this drawing together of the most special, consistent, and intricately related patterns of language in the poem which creates the impression—altogether different from the presentation of the inner life of characters in *Paradise Lost*—that we apprehend Samson's inward experience as if by the unspoken meanings of words, and even finally by silence.

Samson's movement toward his goal in the poem is not the development of an argument, but a growth to be felt, like the silent and unseen growing of his hair. For the blind man, spiritual progress means the re-establishment of the proper relationship between his inward self and the outer world; the indications of his growth are given in his responses to the representatives of that world who confront him with their alien looks and words.

The most obvious signs of Samson's progress toward heroic silence are his increasing imperviousness and his increasing reticence. In the earlier encounters with the Chorus and Manoa he shows a raw vulnerability to the onslaughts of the outside world. He shrinks at the noise of the Chorus approaching, at the sound of his father's name; he expresses horror at the notion of being an object of "gaze," suggesting the sense of being exposed and undefended, open to attack by hostile looks and painful words. Against Dalila he feels he must protect himself almost by physical violence, at least by physical distance: "My Wife, my Traytress, let her not come near me" [725]. But this defence marks the growth of his heroic imperviousness. There is new energy in his voice showing a new relation to the world outside himself. Now he begins to use his separation from the world as a defense, guarding against sensations which might penetrate from without, turning the prison of his inward self once more into a fortress. His blindness shields him from Dalila's "beauty" which, as the Chorus at the close of the episode observes, "though injurious, hath strange power" [1003], yet the sightlessness which shuts out her appearance leaves him especially vulnerable in his responsiveness to touch and sound, through which the outside world can still attack him. He must guard against such violation for,

as he said earlier of his own susceptibility, in words
which recall the metaphor of the "fort":

What boots it at one gate to make defence,
And at another to let in the foe
Effeminatly vanquish't?   [560-562]

To defend himself against touch he uses distance, in
the first words of the episode; at its close, when against
Dalila's knowing plea, "Let me approach at least, and
touch thy hand" [951], he protects himself:

Not for thy life, lest fierce remembrance wake
My sudden rage to tear thee joint by joint.
At distance I forgive thee, go with that . . .
                                          [952-954]

Against her words, and there are many of them, he
has the armor of experience: "Out, out *Hyæna;* these
are thy wonted arts" [748]. Because he is no longer
confused by the sight of her beauty or the touch of
her body, he can hear her words undistracted, as the
reader hears them, stripped of their "false pretexts
and varnish'd colours" [901]. He can "fence" himself against them and repel them for what they are:

      . . . I know thy trains
Though dearly to my cost, thy ginns, and toyls;
Thy fair enchanted cup, and warbling charms
No more on me have power, their force is null'd,
So much of Adders wisdom I have learn't
To fence my ear against thy sorceries.   [932-937]

His freedom from such distraction is emphasized by
his final exchange in this scene with the Chorus. When

they remark on the power of beauty to regain "Love once possest" [1005], Samson points out their susceptibility to the deceits of looks and words with a correction whose acerbity is almost satirical:

> Love-quarrels oft in pleasing concord end,
> Not wedlock-trechery endangering life.
>
> [1008-1009]

By achieving this imperviousness he has made the prison of himself once more a "fort of silence." Words cannot reach him now, not because he is helplessly locked into his own being, but because he actively guards against violation from the world outside himself. His separateness now means invulnerability. He is, as Dalila recognizes, not only blind but deaf to the world—political, social, domestic—where she belongs:

> I see thou art implacable, more deaf
> To prayers, then winds and seas, yet winds to seas
> Are reconcil'd at length, and Sea to Shore:
> Thy anger, unappeasable, still rages,
> Eternal tempest never to be calm'd.   [960-964]

Samson's restored defences are then tested by Harapha, and found to be impregnable. He is indifferent now to the outside world: "Or peace or not, alike to me he comes" [1074]. Because his inner defenses are restored, he feels no longer imprisoned but safely entrenched, for he invites Harapha to "Some narrow place enclos'd" [1117] where confinement will be the blind man's advantage. He is invulnerable to touch, even to the "gaze" of those who can look at him as an object of pity or scorn:

> Cam'st thou for this, vain boaster, to survey me,
> To descant on my strength, and give thy verdit?
> Come nearer, part not hence so slight inform'd;
> But take good heed my hand survey not thee.
>
> [1227-1230]

Language is the ineffectual weapon of the "Tongue-doubtie," to be dismissed with a satirical play on the word "survey," an almost flippant freedom with speech suggested also by his earlier punning on the word "taste" [1091]. Samson confidently claims that his hand with one blow can do more than all Harapha's insulting looks and words.

If the "fort of silence" is to be held once it has been recaptured, Samson must learn not only to keep words out but to give none away. He must become reticent as well as impervious, mute as well as deaf. His experience must escape, as it were, the limitations of human language, as he learns to apprehend in it the special kind of unspoken metaphorical meanings which the reader has recognized from the beginning but which Samson can hear only when he has finally shut out the sound of "talk," "Tongue-batteries," and his own "garrulity." This achievement of silence is revealed to the reader in the last two episodes of the poem, Samson's confrontation with the Officer and the Messenger's report of his death.

The scene with the Officer is the most extraordinary in the work, as Milton exploits most fully the form of a dramatic rather than a narrative poem, to be read rather than performed. Here large changes occur within Samson which direct the total course and meaning of the action, and yet very little is said about them. (The effect is something like that of the final scenes in *Hamlet*, where we sense profound changes in the inner life of the hero which are neither described nor dramatized. But in Milton's poem the changes are wrought instantaneously within a single scene.) There is of course no narrator to interpret them, nor are we invited to visualize in any detail the actions, gestures, or expressions that might explain them. There are no interpretive remarks by the other characters to guide us, and above all, Samson himself gives none of his usual recitations of feelings. Although in the beginning of the episode Samson's decisions are explained— his refusal to perform for his enemies and his reasons for refusing—when his feelings change he gives no explanation to the Chorus. Nor is any cause for the shift provided in the action, least of all in the words of the other characters, to which Samson does not respond. He announces his intentions with apparently calculated inscrutability:

> Be of good courage, I begin to feel
> Some rouzing motions in me which dispose
> To something extraordinary my thoughts.
> I with this Messenger will go along,
> Nothing to do, be sure, that may dishonour
> Our Law, or stain my vow of *Nazarite*.
> If there be aught of presage in the mind,
> This day will be remarkable in my life
> By some great act, or of my days the last.
>
> [1381-1389]

By comparison with his earlier revelations of feeling, this speech is reticent indeed. Without the least show of indecisiveness, it is full of vague terms with unspecified references: "Some," "something," "Nothing," "aught," "some." Although he claims to be describing his "thoughts," he actually tells only how he will

immediately act. That is the sole one of his statements
the Chorus can understand, while by contrast the
reader, knowing the divinely appointed end of Samson's story, possesses his "presage of mind." It is almost as if we now shared an unspoken secret with him.

This sense of sharing with Samson the knowledge
of what is not said is increased by his next speech, when
he deliberately deceives the Officer:

> Because they shall not trail me through thir streets
> Like a wild Beast, I am content to go.
> Masters commands come with a power resistless
> To such as owe them absolute subjection;
> And for a life who will not change his purpose?
> (So mutable are all the ways of men) ...
>   [1402-1407]

Here is more than reticence, it is lying; but the reader,
who shares Samson's unspoken knowledge, is not deceived. We know that he is truly "content to go" for
other reasons than he asserts, or rather, know that his
assertions have metaphorical meanings now intended
by him, which are unheard by the other characters. We
understand him now to be consciously obeying other
commands than his statement seems to indicate, from
another Master, to save a different kind of life. We
recognize that he knows the ways of men to be "mutable" because "rouzing motions" from an immutable
source can change them. We also understand the reason
for his lying. It is a defence, another step in his progress toward the perfect achievement of his heroic goal,
command of the "fort of silence."

The last step "onward" is marked by Samson's
final words, which the reader does not hear directly
from him, but only through the bewildered report of

the Messenger, who merely tells what he has heard without recognizing its meanings. Samson's last speech is a remarkable climax to Milton's presentation of the story from Judges:

> Hitherto, Lords, what your commands impos'd
> I have perform'd, as reason was, obeying,
> Not without wonder or delight beheld.
> Now of my own accord such other tryal
> I mean to shew you of my strength, yet greater;
> As with amaze shall strike all who behold.
>   [1640-1645]

The brilliantly calculated effects of this speech in the poem are made clearer if it is compared with Samson's final words in the Old Testament version of the story:[16]

> . . . O Lord God, remember me, I pray thee, and strengthen me, I pray thee, only this once, O God, that I may be at once avenged of the Philistines for my two eyes.   [Judges xvi: 28]

The savagery of this private vengefulness would obviously be out of key in *Samson Agonistes* (although Milton's Samson shows no more concern to liberate his nation by his final act than does the Biblical Samson) but there is another omission which is more telling. Also absent from Milton's version of the speech is any form of prayer, or declaration of faith, or hymn of praise, any claim by Samson to be God's instrument, or hint of his restored sense of divine favor, such as he gave earlier to Harapha [1140]. Nothing of the hero's inward experience is revealed to his listeners by his suavely courteous manner, which only the reader, knowing the promised end of the story, can recognize to be intentionally ironic, even grimly joking. For we alone recognize Samson's pun on the word "strike" of the last line, by which he means at once that his strength will strike the spectators with amazement, and that they will be amazed by the fact that his strength will strike them down.[17]

In contrast with the restless and broken cadences of Samson's private lament at the beginning of the poem, the detached, controlled irony of his public speeches in the final episodes is a measure of his progress towards his heroic goal of silence. He uses words with his characteristic sense of their inappropriateness to his inward experience, but now he chooses them *because* they are irrelevant, and therefore can mislead men who belong to the outward world and who apprehend only the immediate, ordinary human references of language. Now Samson with calculated rhetorical skill offers those literal meanings to his listeners while he himself intends his words metaphorically. The language of his final speeches therefore marks his movement "onward" in another sense, for now Samson has learned to recognize in his immediate experiences a different order of meanings. He has learned to hear, as it were, the unspoken significance of his words.

The Messenger unknowingly reveals that Samson at last reaches total imperviousness and total reticence. Standing exposed as a "spectacle" before all his enemies, he is indifferent to their staring and beyond reach of their words. They can watch, like the Messenger, as Samson bows his head with "eyes fast fixt . . . as one who pray'd,/ Or some great matter in his mind revolv'd" [1637-1638], but cannot guess the object of his blank gaze. Inviolate to the human world outside himself, he reveals to it nothing of his inner world, so that other men, who depend on sight and hearing, are de-

ceived by his appearance and his speech. He is to them
totally unknowable because he is blind, deaf and mute.
The mighty crash with which he pulls the theatre down
declares his command for eternity of the "fort of
silence."

The achievement is absolute. With his final act,
Samson passes beyond the visible world, beyond human
society, ultimately beyond definition even by the metaphorical meanings of language. He becomes in one
sense a mere body, a totally insensate and inscrutable
object, impervious alike to ministrations and to honors,
unheeding of "silent obsequie" or the tribute of "copi-
ous Legend, or sweet Lyric Song" [1732, 1737]. In
another sense he becomes a force of nature, equally
unfeeling and unknowable:

> This utter'd, straining all his nerves he bow'd,
> As with the force of winds and waters pent,
> When Mountains tremble, those two massie Pillars
> With horrible convulsion to and fro,
> He tugg'd, he shook, till down they came and drew
> The whole roof after them, with burst of thunder
> Upon the heads of all who sate beneath . . .
>   [1646-1652]

He is likened to "an ev'ning Dragon" swooping upon
his prey, "an Eagle/ His cloudless thunder bolted on
thir heads," a phoenix, a "Holocaust" [1690-1707].[18]
He has become the inhuman power that Dalila feared,
now truly "inflexible as steel" [816], now literally "implacable, more deaf/ To prayers, then winds and seas,"
unappeasable as an "Eternal tempest never to be
calm'd" [960-964]. He has passed beyond the reach of
all social and political relationships[19]—with parent or
wife, with friends, countrymen or enemies—to become

now utterly "separate to God" [31] but in a communion that denies definition not only by Manoa's conventional tributes, or by heroic "Fame" which even Dalila, despite her worldly ambitions, recognizes to be "double-mouth'd" [971]. He has escaped definition even by the metaphorical language used until now to represent his experience. Such Biblical phraseology, such traditional Christian images for the spiritual rewards of the faithful no longer seem appropriate to define Samson's end, as if he were not a son returning home to his divine Father, a soul to its Maker, a saint to Heaven, but a "Plant;/ Select, and Sacred" [362-363] returning in wordless unconsciousness to the soil which nourished it.[20] He has reached his final "rest," which is not the reward of Lycidas "In the blest Kingdoms meek of joy and love" [177] nor of Adam and Eve guided by Providence to choose their "place of rest" in the world [XII, 647]. Samson's "rest" is a kind of negation of human experience, an obliteration of the self. It is the achievement of a silent communion with God alone—Samson is never once in the poem heard to pray—uttered only in the wordless language of "intimate impulse," "Divine impulsion," "divine instinct," "rouzing motions." [21] It is like a strange transformation into another order of being, no longer "mutable," almost as if he passed into the living body of God, "Whose ear is ever open; and his eye/ Gracious to re-admit the suppliant" [1172-1173]. Its closest literary parallel is the apotheosis of the hero at the end of *Œdipus at Colonus,* the miraculous transformation of a man into a kind of deity, a mystery beyond human apprehension, marked by thunder and concluding in secrecy and silence. But Samson is not apotheosized into a spirit who will watch over the affairs of men as Œdipus is made a guiding genius for Athens, or as Lycidas becomes the "Genius of the shore" guarding "all that wander in that perilous flood" [183-185].[22] Samson is transported beyond those human concerns. Nor for him is there an ultimate promise, as there is for Adam and Eve, of "New Heav'ns, new Earth, Ages of endless date/ Founded in righteousness and peace and love" [XII, 549-550]. For him the promised end is oblivion, the "benumming Opium" of death for which he once longed [630], the "close" of all his miseries "and the balm" [651].

This escape from the world of men, from language, finally from all human experience, is the heroic triumph honored by the poem. It is the fulfillment of Samson's unique destiny, for which he was specially elected, the reconquest of the "fort of silence" entrusted to him alone. The magnitude of the accomplishment is the mark of his heroic nature. Yet Milton's presentation of the story, for all its acknowledgement of Samson's "separateness," does not allow us to understand the morality of his achievement as God's plan only for his chosen heroes (in the way the Chorus, imitating Greek choral odes, contrasts the destiny of those who have been "solemnly elected,/ . . . To some great work" with the fate of the nameless "common rout," 674-680). Samson's "separateness" itself, his "impotence," his blindness, his imprisonment, his "fort of silence" have all finally been transformed from facts of unique individual experience into metaphors for the human condition, for the relationship of the private self to the world of men and to God. This figurative interpretation of his experience sets Samson apart from the other characters in the poem, who cannot share it, but not from the reader, who understands the facts of Samson's story to be metaphorically meaningful precisely because he recognizes them to stand for the human condition. It is this recognition which makes it possible for him to be drawn into special intimacy with the protagonist.

The peculiar uses of language invented by Milton to describe the inward experience of his hero appear to be directed to the solitary reader stripped in so far as possible of his social identity. They seem to be dependent on elemental feelings which we can experience with Samson in so far as we are human. They create the impression that we share with him an understanding of unutterable "motions" within his most private self. Paradoxically, therefore, when Samson escapes finally even his wordless intimacy with the reader, as he passes beyond the reach even of elemental feelings into a condition no longer human, we may interpret this too as a universally applicable metaphor for the final step toward the "rest" which is the goal of all men. In the oblivion of death Samson achieves the condition of "silence" identified in Milton's poem with perfect freedom from the "mutable . . . ways of men."

The ultimate paradox, then, is the poem itself. As in *Paradise Lost,* Milton in *Samson Agonistes* shapes his Biblical material into a legend of the morality of language. Both the epic and the dramatic poem describe the chaos wrought by violation of divinely ordained uses of words and celebrate the final restoration of order through man's proper form of utterance re-established. In *Paradise Lost* it is eloquence which is restored and poetry which is its triumphant instrument in the moral redemption of society. But in *Samson Agonistes* the hero's achievement is a denial of the moral ordering of society and in one sense of poetry. Samson's conquest of the "fort of silence" makes all forms of human communion and articulation irrelevant, as Manoa's conventional eulogy spoken for the dead hero (like all his earlier speeches about Samson) with its promise of literary fame is supremely irrelevant to the self which has become like an unconscious object or force of nature. All that can appropriately be said at the end of the poem is that some "unsearchable" pattern has been completed "in the close," "unexpectedly," according to God's "uncontroulable intent" [1746-1754]. Its witnesses have been granted a "new acquist/ Of true experience from this great event" [1755-1756], but true "experience" has been defined in *Samson Agonistes* as utterly inward, "Inseparably dark," secret, wordless, and finally inhuman.[23] The poem itself therefore paradoxically denies the power of eloquence, of literature, which must inevitably be bound by the limits of language and of all things human, at the same time that it creates a vision of those limits heroically transcended. In this effort, *Samson Agonistes* prepares the way, not for Pope, but for Wordsworth. When Samson triumphantly escapes from human life "As with the force of winds and waters pent,/ When mountains tremble," he is recognizable as the ancestor of a kind of Wordsworthian hero, a poetic celebration of wordless and immutable non-human nature.[24]

II

"THE WORLD WELL LOST"

When Milton in *Samson Agonistes* invented a
language very different from his epic manner, he used
it to express antithetical attitudes. Although the work
is modelled in its outlines and in many conventional
details on Greek tragedy, it seems purposely to alter
the function of that form—originally evolved for performance before vast public audiences as part of a
national and religious festival—in order to appeal to
the solitary reader's feelings, to evoke his most private
and inward responses in so far as possible abstracted
from or lifted out of his identity in the social world.
The style seems designed, then, not to accumulate the
wealth of associations conserved in literary and social
language, but to lay bare some irreducible core of
meaning. It insists upon the truth of a vision which
finally escapes articulation. This effect is more extreme
than the efforts of earlier religious poets, of Herbert,
for example, or Marvell in "The Coronet," whose
search for a sacred language purified of literary and

social profanations implies some recognition of the limitations of all human utterance. The view of the morality of language expressed in *Samson Agonistes* goes beyond distrust of human speech to renunciation of it as the chief threat to the soul's proper, silent communion with God. The limits of language are not bounds appropriate to man's creaturely nature, as Herbert accepts them, or as Raphael defines them to Adam,[1] but violations of his essential identity, his wordless, inward self. The poet's function, then, is not as Herbert might intend, to learn a purified language suited for conversing with God, but to invent a style closer to the poetic aims of Traherne, who celebrated "Dumnesse" as the state of innocence, which surmounts the limits of language to recreate perfect silence.

Dryden never fully explored the implications of this view, but the parallels we shall find with *Samson Agonistes* in *All for Love* show that he strongly felt their attraction. In that play he creates a situation and characters virtually abstracted from the particularities of setting so richly exploited in his Shakespearean model, portrayed in a language largely stripped of the social accents so precise in his own satirical style, as if to examine human society in its fundamental patterns, human feelings reduced to their essential elements.[2] The image which he then lays bare in the play, for all its inconsistencies, is of a world in which relationships are meaningless and feelings inexpressible because finally dependent on language which is both arbitrary and threatening. This world, the main emphasis in the play underlines, it is the hero's achievement to renounce for a state of wordless and unconscious oblivion: Antony escapes, like Samson, into inertness and silence. But his release is more passive than Samson's fierce negation of experience, and the play ends in large confusions which prevent any clear assertion that his death represents an heroic triumph over the limitations of society and all things human. *All for Love* celebrates the world of words well lost, but not the heroic image regained of immutability and silence. It shows Dryden to have been sympathetic with certain attitudes at the heart of Milton's dramatic poem, and the superiority of *All for Love* to all his other plays suggests that his sympathy was deeply felt. Yet the confusions and contradictions in the play also reveal that Dryden never fully apprehended Milton's vision in its magnificent and ferocious clarity.

Dryden's transformation of *Antony and Cleopatra* created in *All for Love* a drama similar in many important ways to *Samson Agonistes*. We shall find that Dryden's presentation of his hero's experience parallels Milton's in its shape and emphasis, in the portrayal of Antony and his relationship to the world outside himself, to which the other characters who confront him belong.

Dryden's Antony suggests comparisons with Samson from the moment of his first appearance (the play's concentration on the hero at the sacrifice of interest in Cleopatra itself resembles Milton's focus more than Shakespeare's). Walking on the scene *"with a disturbed motion,"* Antony seems to soliloquize, although Ventidius is actually present to hear his private lament:

> They tell me, 'tis my birthday, and I'll keep it
> With double pomp of sadness.
> 'Tis what the day deserves, which gave me breath.

Why was I raised the meteor of the world,
Hung in the skies, and blazing as I travelled,
Till all my fires were spent; and then cast downward,
To be trod out by Cæsar?   [I, i, p. 350]

The lines, while more plaintive, less fiercely bitter in
tone, resemble Samson's questioning of his destiny at
the beginning of his soliloquy:

Why was my breeding order'd and prescrib'd
As of a person separate to God,
Design'd for great exploits; if I must dye
Betray'd, Captiv'd, and both my Eyes put out,
Made of my Enemies the scorn and gaze;
To grind in Brazen Fetters under task
With this Heav'n-gifted strength?   [30-36]

The parallels point most obviously to similarities of
situation: both heroes are introduced in their defeat,
which is the more devastating for its contrast with
former greatness. Both recognize themselves to be
somehow "separate" from other men, circling alone
above them like a celestial body or set apart like some
creature of special "breeding." Yet both feel their
unique greatness, as well as their downfall, to have
been imposed upon them by outside forces. In place of
the traditional hero's self-assertive boasting (so often
parodied in Satan's speeches, and more satirically in
Harapha's), instead of claims to autonomous power,
we find characteristic use of the passive voice to describe their own experiences: "raised," "Hung,"
"cast," "trod," and "order'd," "prescrib'd," "Design'd," "Betray'd," "Captiv'd." Each hero represents himself as an object acted upon by powers outside
his own being. This sense of helplessness, a kind of

impotence or inactivity, is used at the beginning of each drama as the sign of the protagonist's defeat, the effect of his surrender to the lesser power of a woman. Ventidius gives such an interpretation of Antony's collapse in one of his earliest speeches contrasting the hero's past with his diminished present, again using words (especially metaphors of bodily mutilation and confinement) resembling some of Samson's own descriptions of his fall:[3]

> I tell thee, eunuch, she has quite unmanned him
> Can any Roman see, and know him now,
> Thus altered from the lord of half mankind,
> Unbent, unsinewed, made a woman's toy,
> Shrunk from the vast extent of all his honours,
> And crampt within a corner of the world?
>
> [I, i, p. 349]

To the single-minded Roman, Antony's present impotence seems to be the result of his abandonment to Cleopatra, its sign his retirement from active leadership to a life of privacy in Egypt. The ultimate cause of this decline he sees in the mixed nature of Antony's character, his own language echoing the hero's sense of himself as a passive figure acted upon more than acting:

> Just, just his nature.
> Virtue's his path; but sometimes 'tis too narrow
> For his vast soul; and then he starts out wide,
> And bounds into a vice, that bears him far
> From his first course, and plunges him in ills:
> But, when his danger makes him find his fault,
> Quick to observe, and full of sharp remorse,

He censures eagerly his own misdeeds,
Judging himself with malice to himself,
And not forgiving what as man he did,
Because his other parts are more than man.—
He must not thus be lost.   [I, i, pp. 347-348]

Ventidius' reading of Antony's "nature" is essen-
tially the same as Plutarch's (according to North's
translation) in *The Life of Marcus Antonius* and as
Dryden's in the play's Preface.[4] He judges him according to the traditional code of values which condemns
passion as it threatens duty, honor, and action. He
views him as a great man who greatly errs, whose
remarkable nature has its special dangers. Ventidius,
then, does not see the hero's state as a reflection of
fundamental qualities of human experience, as Milton
imagines Samson's "separateness" and "impotence"
to be metaphors for the inward self in relation to the
outer world, and finally as images for true heroic
achievement. Yet the main emphasis created by the
style and structure of Dryden's play as a whole, like
Milton's presentation of the Old Testament story,
points to a more complicated and less predictable
morality than Ventidius' explanation offers. *All for
Love,* although it ultimately contradicts itself, leaves
its audience with the image of a hero who is set apart
from the world and yet acted upon by its powers, not
finally as a result of his own actions or even of his
character, but because man's inward being reduced to
its essential core must inevitably stand in such a
relationship to the world which threatens from outside
himself.

In the opening of the play, a vague supernatural
power seems to brood over Antony's world. "Portents
and prodigies," fierce floods, and tidal waves announce

the coming doom of Egypt, seemingly as inevitable as
the passing of ages that transforms the very face of
nature. "Fortune striding, like a vast Colossus"
[I, i, p. 345] is invoked as the ruling power by Romans
as well as Egyptians, and Dryden's transposition of
that image of the Colossus from a metaphor for the
heroic stature of the protagonist (as Shakespeare's
Cleopatra uses it)[5] to a definition of the force said to
direct his destiny, emphasizes the hero's helplessness.
The play also ends with a formal acknowledgement of
the supernatural powers that seem to rule man's life.
Yet the references to these powers often sound like
conventional gestures designed to give an antique
flavor to the language, or like vague admissions of
the incomprehensibility of human affairs. They have
no more convincing force than the claims for the super-
human efficacy of David's speech in *Absalom and
Achitophel* because they do not form a pattern articu-
lating a consistent theory of supernatural authority
over man's existence: such an authority never enters
or alters the course of action in the drama. Fortune
or Fate or Chance therefore does not play a part
comparable to that of Divine Providence in *Samson
Agonistes*. Dryden's drama shows a hero buffeted by
forces outside his own control, and the other characters
less extravagantly demonstrate the same helplessness,
but the language and action of the play locate those
forces in the human, social, political world more often
and more convincingly than in the supernatural. That
world acts upon the hero through the medium of speech,
and in this sense Antony's experience again parallels
Samson's. He too is susceptible to words which wield
their dangerous influence over him with almost the
autonomous force of objects.

Alexas would seem to be the most obvious embodiment of the threatening world acting upon the hero

to shape his destiny. Sharing nothing with Shakespeare's Alexas or his figure of the eunuch, Mardian, Alexas in *All for Love* is made the principal manipulator of the action. He is even the acknowledged director of Cleopatra's behavior [II, i, p. 364], who is therefore herself a totally transformed version of Shakespeare's Egyptian queen. Repeatedly he devises schemes for her to work upon the hero, and it is he, not Cleopatra, who invents the fatal deception of Antony.[6] This Alexas is the familiar traditional figure of the wily courtier or politician, the Machiavel or Achitophel, confessed plotter of self-interested "designs" and "counsels" [I, i, p. 346] who values and lives by "wit" rather than "plain dull virtue" [III, i, p. 391]. His instruments of power are Satanic: a "servile tongue" that speaks "fawning eloquence" [V, i, p. 422], and a "gift of lying" [V, i, p. 423]. His tricks and falsehoods are always revealed to the audience before they are worked upon Antony, so that we can watch his deceptions as they follow the predictable pattern for such a character, with the success expected of the wily hypocrite who traditionally manipulates language to dupe the hero.

A clear example of Alexas' verbal power over Antony is shown in Act IV, when Ventidius, falling himself into the eunuch's trap, tries to make him "speak truth" to Antony about Cleopatra's feelings for Dolabella:

No fine set speech, no cadence, no turned periods,
But a plain homespun truth, is what I ask . . .
                                            [IV, i, p. 408]

What he hears from Alexas, however, is the insinuating flattery of the artful hypocrite, which Antony is unable to recognize:

Alex. As far as love may plead for woman's frailty,
Urged by desert and greatness of the lover,
So far, divine Octavia, may my queen
Stand even excused to you for loving him
Who is your lord: so far, from brave Ventidius,
May her past actions hope a fair report.

Ant. 'Tis well, and truly spoken: mark, Ventidius.

Alex. To you, most noble emperor, her strong passion
Stands not excused, but wholly justified.
Her beauty's charms alone, without her crown,
From Ind and Meroe drew the distant vows
Of sighing kings; and at her feet were laid
The sceptres of the earth, exposed on heaps,
To choose where she would reign:
She thought a Roman only could deserve her,
And, of all Romans, only Antony;
And, to be less than wife to you, disdained
Their lawful passion.

Ant. 'Tis but truth.   [IV, i, p. 409]

Having flattered and confused his listeners, Alexas
inserts with elaborate indirection a hint that we know
to be a lie but that Ventidius believes to be "substan-
tial reason" which he urges Alexas to tell Antony:

    Alex. Else had I never dared to offend his ears
    With what the last necessity has urged
    On my forsaken mistress; yet I must not
    Presume to say, her heart is wholly altered.
                                [IV, i, p. 410]

Antony not only fails to recognize and dismiss the deception; he fears the eunuch's words as if they were
weapons of killing power:

    Ant. No, dare not for thy life, I charge thee dare
      not
Pronounce that fatal word!   [IV, i, p. 410]

The hero is helpless in the toils of Alexas' rhetoric, easily manipulated by the schemer's conventional verbal tools of flattery, distorted logic, and lies.

Although Dryden found no such figure in Shakespeare's *Antony and Cleopatra,* he created in Alexas a familiar dramatic type, whose role as manipulator of other men follows a recognizable literary tradition. Alexas' power over Antony, through his own artful use of language and through the enactment of his plots by Cleopatra—also said to wield a formidable gift of "eloquence" [IV, i, p. 404]—[7] is not then in itself profoundly revealing of the reinterpretation expressed in Dryden's revision of *Antony and Cleopatra.* In its outlines, the expanded role of Alexas merely seems to follow a different set of theatrical conventions than Dryden found in the original tragedy. It suggests *Othello* as a model, for example, or plays of Marston and Webster, indicating perhaps that Dryden was attracted to this dramatic tradition by an early interest in the power of the crooked politician, later to be expanded in his satirical portrait of Shaftesbury.

What is more revealing is that within the total design of the work, Alexas' function does not actually follow the pattern to be predicted from his conventional characterization, because that pattern is altered in important ways by its relation to the roles of other figures in the play. That is to say, it is expected that the Satanic, Achitophel figure be able to act upon the hero (the way Iago manipulates Othello, for example, or Archimago in Book I of *The Faerie Queene* dupes the Red Cross Knight) through the power of his language,

as does Alexas in the scene in which he stirs Antony
to jealousy. But the meaning of that manipulation is
entirely altered when we find other characters, representing quite other conventional types, wielding virtually the same controlling influence over the protagonist, and with instruments of verbal power. A quite different notion of the hero's nature is implied, a different
understanding of his relationship to the world of men
and therefore to language. It is within this context that
Alexas' manipulation of Antony may be interpreted.

When the play opens, we are presented with the
figure of Alexas plotting his "designs" in order to
keep Antony in Egypt. Ventidius' entrance is then
announced,[8] and from the first descriptions we see
him as a recognizable opposite to the wily politician.
Even Alexas, his "mortal foe," acknowledges his
"worth":

A braver Roman never drew a sword;
Firm to his prince, but as a friend, not slave.
He ne'er was of his pleasures; but presides
O'er all his cooler hours, and morning counsels:
In short, the plainness, fierceness, rugged virtue,
Of an old true-stampt Roman lives in him.
[I, i, p. 346-347]

We recognize a type which includes Shakespeare's own
Ventidius but especially his Enobarbus, the honest
soldier whose blunt speech is free of artful calculation
(it is the role played by Iago to dupe his victims), and
the expectations aroused by this type are fulfilled in
the opening of the first scene between Ventidius and
Antony. After the manner of Kent with King Lear,
Ventidius exercises his sincerity by criticizing his
master:

Are you Antony?
I'm liker what I was, than you to him
I left you last.　　　　　　　　　　[I, i, p. 352]

Throughout the scene he claims the "privilege of plain
love to speak" [I, i, p. 357], earning by his forthright
remarks the anger and insults of Antony, who cannot
bear to hear what he says about Cleopatra. Ventidius'
honest words, his direct appeals—"Up, up, for honour's
sake" [I, i, p. 355]—seem to have no influence upon the
hero. Yet in the course of the scene Antony is suddenly
won to the Roman's cause, and by a speech of Ventidius' which calls attention to his uses of language in
ways different from his usual "plain" style:

Vent. No prince but you
Could merit that sincerity I used,
Nor durst another man have ventured it;
But you, ere love misled your wandering eyes,
Were sure the chief and best of human race,
Framed in the very pride and boast of nature;
So perfect, that the gods, who formed you, wondered
At their own skill, and cried—A lucky hit
Has mended our design. Their envy hindered,
Else you had been immortal, and a pattern,
When Heaven would work for ostentation's sake
To copy out again.
　　Ant. But Cleopatra—
Go on; for I can bear it now.
　　Vent. No more.
　　Ant. Thou dar'st not trust my passion, but thou
　　　　may'st;
Thou only lov'st, the rest have flattered me.
　　Vent. Heaven's blessing on your heart for that kind
　　　　word!
May I believe you love me? Speak again.

Ant. Indeed I do. Speak this, and this, and this.
　　[*Hugging him.*
Thy praises were unjust; but, I'll deserve them,
And yet mend all. Do with me what thou wilt;
Lead me to victory! thou know'st the way.
　　　　　　　　　　　　　　　[I, i, pp. 358-359]

　　If Ventidius' established character for truthfulness and Antony's historical reputation for greatness
(or Shakespeare's familiar version of it) prevent us
from hearing Ventidius' extended praises as mere flattery, such as we expect from Alexas, we at least find
them elaborately figurative and hyperbolical, in contrast with his habitual manner of speaking. For the
first time, Ventidius' speech does not express the qualities associated with his character. In fact, these lines
seem to bear virtually no relation to his typical mode of
expression. They seem to exist almost autonomously
as a "set-piece," an example of effective rhetoric. And
Antony appears to be very susceptible to this language: he is instantly converted. He now urges Ventidius to go on speaking, accepts his claims to honesty
and surrenders himself entirely to the Roman's cause.
The speech itself seems to have a mysterious power
over him. He appears almost hypnotized by the sound
of the words without regard to their meanings. Having
just heard himself described in the most extravagant
terms, he instantly distinguishes Ventidius as the one
man who has never "flattered" him (a remark which
may refer more generally to the soldier's manner but
must also include his immediately preceding hyperboles) and then four lines later refers to the same
speech as "unjust" and undeserved praise. This apparent contradiction suggests that Antony is moved as
if by the sound of Ventidius' words more than their
meaning. It does not precisely matter to him whether

the description is true or falsely flattering; he is over-come by it. Yet its power also seems independent of any appeal to definable emotions, to Antony's ambi-tion or love of power and excitement or sense of honor or simple energy. He gives himself up after Ventidius' speech almost with indifference—"Do with me what thou wilt"—and his return to the role of military gen-eral, of Emperor, is a surrender of his will to the per-suasive power of words themselves, as if without regard to the values they express.

This first encounter between the hero and another character who acts upon him is extremely curious in itself, and especially surprising as an exchange between Ventidius, Alexas' opposite, and the hero. Ventidius, we have been told (and the assertion is in harmony with the tradition to which the characterization belongs), is an honest man. Not for him the schemer's manipula-tion of language to bend other men to his own pur-poses. He judges by deeds rather than talk: "Words, words; but Actium, sir; remember Actium" [II, i, p. 374]. He claims only the "privilege of plain love to speak" and that plainness is the antithesis of Alexas' devious rhetoric and of Cleopatra's "charms," which like Dalila's are chiefly verbal and associated by Ven-tidius himself with the enchanting eloquence of the Sirens [IV, i, p. 404]. Yet in the very first exchange we see Ventidius uncharacteristically wielding rhetorical power in a speech which effects an almost magical con-version of Antony. The implication is that the hero's susceptibility to language is more special and puzzling than would be suggested, in the scene quoted earlier, by his far more conventionally predictable failure to un-tangle the devious rhetoric of Alexas.

This first exchange with Ventidius is the paradigm of later encounters between Antony and the other characters, who work upon him with their words.[9]

Again and again he is made to shift his allegiance, as Shakespeare's Antony vascillates between the conflicting appeals of Egypt and Rome. But in Dryden's play these changes have the curiously unmotivated quality of the first instantaneous conversion. The hero seems to be acted upon by forces entirely outside himself, which reach him as words wielding autonomous power.

Octavia and her supporters effect one of these transformations of Antony's allegiance in Act III. When she unexpectedly appears, Antony first repulses her with the unkind title of "Cæsar's sister" [III, i, p. 387] and they argue their grievances. Yet after she offers to pretend a reconciliation, retaining only the "barren name of wife" [p. 388], we are told that some change in feeling occurs within Antony, who blushes "To be outdone in generosity" and "winks" to hide a tear. He still refuses to yield to her, "For I can ne'er be conquered but by love;/ And you do all for duty" [p. 389], although when she hints that she does indeed love him he is further moved:

> O Dolabella, which way shall I turn?
> I find a secret yielding in my soul;
> But Cleopatra, who would die with me,
> Must she be left? Pity pleads for Octavia;
> But does it not plead more for Cleopatra?
> [III, i, p. 389]

His moment of conversion comes, however, not precisely as if he were persuaded by Octavia's pleading, but only when all the characters in the scene bombard him with a peal of titles: "Emperor!" "Friend!" "Husband!" "Father!" [p. 390].[10] Then his capitulation is complete, and expressed with the same almost careless indifference as his earlier surrender to Ventidius:

I am vanquished: take me,
Octavia; take me, children; share me all.
[III, i, p. 390]

And finally to Octavia:

This is thy triumph; lead me where thou wilt;
Even to thy brother's camp.   [III, i, p. 391]

He relinquishes his will to hers, turns himself over to the enemy, even willingly embraces imprisonment, like Samson in the opening episodes, as if abandoning his body to the humiliations of captivity.

Outlined in this way, the scene may seem to prepare for the change in Antony by more gradual steps than can be traced in the first encounter with Ventidius, but these gradations are presented in terms as odd as those depicting the final moment of conversion; like that climax, the changes in feeling said to precede it are suggestive of the hero's helplessness to resist the power of language. First his shifting sympathies are indicated only by signs such as an actor might give to represent emotions: Antony blushes, he blinks away an unexplained tear. Then his own speech announces what he feels—"Pity pleads for Octavia"—but in a metaphor which locates his emotions outside himself. "Pity" is a suppliant who approaches to beg, or a lawyer who argues a case, an allegorical figure strangely dissociated both from Octavia, who is meant to occasion the pity, and from Antony, who is said to feel it.[11] Even his capitulation seems independent of the emotion for his wife which the encounter has supposedly aroused. Although he claims that she can conquer him only by love, he succumbs finally to a rehearsal of titles which, but for her ritualistic invocation of the name for a category of relationship—"Husband!"—are not in-

dications of Octavia's love for Antony, nor appeals to
answering feelings in him. When he surrenders, then,
it is as if to the power of the words themselves, rather
than to the driving force of passions within himself—
love and pity for his wife and children (of which earlier in the play there have been no signs) or ambition
and loyalty (the emotions to be stirred by "Emperor!"
and "Friend!" yet actually irrelevant to the particular
inner conflict said to be felt and acted out in this scene).
He is vanquished by the names as if they were abstract
or impersonal categories, detached as much from the
people who speak them as from himself.

One other scene in which Antony experiences instantaneous conversion shows even more emphatically
the hero's curious relationship to language. Antony,
who believes that Cleopatra has betrayed him, has
again aligned himself with Ventidius, until he receives
from Alexas a description of her supposed death.
He is characteristically at the mercy of this verbal
deception and, after hearing Alexas' lies, immediately announces yet another transformation of his
feelings:

> Then art thou innocent, my poor dear love?
> And art thou dead?
> O those two words! their sound should be divided:
> Hadst thou been false, and died; or hadst thou lived,
> And hadst been true—But innocence and death!
> This shows not well above. Then what am I,
> The murderer of this truth, this innocence!
> Thoughts cannot form themselves in words so horrid
> As can express my guilt!   [V, i, p. 426]

We could dismiss the passage as meaninglessly bad
writing if we could simply say that Dryden intended
to make the speech express Antony's emotions at this

heightened moment, but instead made the hero merely talk about those emotions. The lines cannot be so easily ignored, however, because they are at once strikingly odd and yet finally representative of language as it is used elsewhere in the play. Antony does not even seem to be talking here about his emotions: he is talking about language. Attention is directed away from the hero's feelings and even from the discovered qualities in Cleopatra which are said to have aroused those feelings. The lines focus instead first upon the phrase "those two words," then upon Antony's concern with their placing in the grammar of his first sentence and with their "sound." When he reaches his confession of "guilt," again his attention is given to finding words for it, or rather to the failure of "Thoughts," existing as it were outside himself, to find them. The transformation of Antony in this scene again appears to be wrought by the power of words themselves as abstract sounds or names for impersonal categories of experience. It is as if he is moved by the actual syllables "innocence," "death," "guilt." His attention is absorbed by words, and the effect of focusing on them in this fashion is to isolate them from their meanings, as if they were neutral sounds that exert power independently of the attitudes, values, or feelings of the speaker or the listener. Their influence seems to derive from their very arbitrariness. In one sense, then, *All for Love* predicts attitudes toward language that we have found in Milton's presentation of Satan and in *Absalom and Achitophel*: the play opens with a vision of Antony's world in chaos, where words have become severed from original or authoritatively sanctioned meanings:

Portents and prodigies have grown so frequent,
That they have lost their name. [I, i, p. 343]

In a more important sense, Antony's relationship to the world and therefore to language suggests comparisons with Samson's. As we have seen, each hero is represented as separate from his world, yet threatened in a series of encounters with its representatives—the other figures in the play—who would act upon his inward self through his susceptibility to language.

The power of the world's instrument, language, is expressed in *All for Love* by many devices of style, as well as by particular allusions, recalling Milton's special language in *Samson Agonistes*. These borrowings, supported by other related expressive patterns in the play, present a view of experience which is never consistently worked out, but which in important respects resembles closely Milton's in *Samson Agonistes*. Whether or not Dryden was at any point in *All for Love* knowingly imitating Milton's poem, the similarities between the two works deny the separation of their authors into "worlds apart."

Even the passages quoted so far have given illustration of the frequency with which the characters in Dryden's play mention "words," "names," "titles," "syllables," "speech," "eloquence," "hearing," "sounds." Such references are combined, as in *Samson Agonistes*, with habitual naming of the actual organs of speaking and listening, sometimes in phrases which might have the effect of merely conventional formulas if they were not so often repeated: "Nor meant my words should reach your ears" [I, i, p. 344]; "never more/ Shall that sound reach my ears" [I, i, p. 353]; "To my ears, the message sounds" [II, i, p. 364]; "abuse your ears" [IV, i, p. 408]; "offend his ears" [IV, i. p. 410]; and similarly, "Curse on the tongue that bids this general joy!" [I, i, p. 348]; "I

allow your tongue free license" [I, i, p. 357] ; "I dare
not trust my tongue to tell her so" [IV, i, p. 395] ;
"Save thy base tongue its office" [V, i, p. 425].

The effect of this stylistic device, combined as we
shall see with other uses of language reminiscent of
Milton's dramatic poem, is to endow words with tangible properties almost as palpably physical as the
tongues that speak them and the ears that receive
them. In one speech, which resembles two separate
passages of *Samson Agonistes,* Ventidius, refusing to
"curse" Antony, instead offers words as soothing
medicine :[12]

> You are too sensible already
> Of what you've done, too conscious of your failings ;
> And, like a scorpion, whipt by others first
> To fury, sting yourself in mad revenge.
> I would bring balm, and pour it in your wounds,
> Cure your distempered mind, and heal your fortunes.
> [I, i, pp. 354-355]

Far more often, as in Milton's poem, words in *All for
Love* are imagined as dangerous objects, weapons, with
power to wound the ears of the listener. In another
passage, for example, Antony's phrasing resembles
Samson's defense against Dalila's verbal power : "So
much of Adders wisdom I have learn't/ To fence my
ear against thy sorceries" [936-937]. Dryden's parallel lines also make the temptress a Siren whose words
are endowed with physical properties, as if they were
weapons or poison that could penetrate Antony's body :

> I must not hear you.
> I have a fool within me takes your part ;
> But honour stops my ears. [IV, i, p. 416]

Here the hero's instrument of defense is itself a word, "honour," that has metaphorical weight and volume as if it were an object. Elsewhere, Antony laments, "How many deaths are in this word, *Depart*" [IV, i, p. 395], and urges Dolabella in delivering his message to "Take off the edge from every sharper sound" [IV, i, p. 396]. Cleopatra feels *"Depart"* to be a "rugged word" [IV, i, p. 401], "perish" a "hard word" [II, i, p. 374], "Octavia" a "fatal name" [III, i, p. 392]. In the same metaphorical pattern, words can harm the speaker as well as the listener. Dolabella defends his chiding of Antony: "each word I speak/ Stabs my own heart, before it reach your ear" [III, i, p. 384], and with more grotesquely physical imagery, Antony refuses to beg pardon of Cæsar:

> No; that word,
> Forgive, would choke me up,
> And die upon my tongue.   [III, i, p. 387]

Throughout the play, metaphors endowing words with the solidity of objects emphasize their dangerous power. These figures therefore suggest that, like Samson's, Antony's susceptibility to language—not only to the calculated rhetoric of Alexas but to the seemingly autonomous power of words themselves—is not uniquely characteristic of his individual nature, but is expressive of the inevitable relationship of the human self to the world outside, whose principle means of attack is language.

Indeed this point is emphasized by the fact that other figures in *All for Love* show a similar susceptibility. Particularly this is true when the characters are driven to speech by what are represented to be sudden bursts of feeling. At such moments we recognize that the characters do experience emotional disturbances, yet this recognition does not mitigate our sense that they express their feelings in a strange way. For example, Ventidius in the first encounter with Antony:

> *Vent.* You may kill me;
> You have done more already,—called me traitor.
>
> *Ant.* Art thou not one?
>
> *Vent.* For showing you yourself,
> Which none else durst have done? but had I been
> That name, which I disdain to speak again,
> I needed not have sought your abject fortunes,
> Come to partake your fate, to die with you.
> What hindered me to have led my conquering eagles
> To fill Octavius' bands? I could have been
> A traitor then, a glorious, happy traitor,
> And not have been so called.   [I, i, pp. 357-358]

Or at the moment of Ventidius' death:

> Now, farewell, emperor!—
> Methinks that word's too cold to be my last:
> Since death sweeps all distinctions, farewell, friend!
>   [V, i, p. 429]

At another such crisis of heightened emotion Cleopatra speaks in the same manner:

> Is that a word
> For Antony to use to Cleopatra?
> O that faint word, *respect*! how I disdain it!
> Disdain myself, for loving after it!
> He should have kept that word for cold Octavia.
>   [II, i, p. 363]

Like Antony, the other characters in the play seem almost hypnotized by words as independent entities.

If words, especially those which traditionally have moral and psychological connotations—such as "innocence," "guilt," "honour," "traitor," "friend," "respect"—have the autonomous, physical identity and force of objects, they derive these qualities from what we have called their arbitrariness, their own essential neutrality. They are not creations of God infused with meanings by their divine origins, like the language of Milton's unfallen men and angels. They are instruments or counters in a seemingly arbitrary system of exchange, existing independently like objects, without any evidently necessary connection with human values, or emotions, or even actions. They operate according to certain rules, as do the units in any system; but the rules themselves dictate arbitrary patterns. Words function according to the laws of grammar, of rhetoric, of "style," rather than as the expression of ideas or feelings, the means of communion. The characters therefore speak them as a performer in a play repeats his lines, and are recognized to be acting out parts with which prescribed "styles" are associated. This metaphor is used first in the exchange between Ventidius and Antony, which in so many of its details exemplifies the pattern of succeeding scenes:

Ant. Sure there's contagion in the tears of friends:
See, I have caught it too. Believe me, 'tis not
For my own griefs, but thine.—Nay, father!

Vent. Emperor.

Ant. Emperor! Why, that's the style of victory;
The conqu'ring soldier, red with unfelt wounds,
Salutes his general so: but never more
Shall that sound reach my ears.   [I, i, p. 353]

As in the other scenes representing sudden emotional crises and conversions, the focus is shifted here from feelings and values to words. Antony's attention is given to Ventidius' "style" of speaking, which is associated with a formal title, "Emperor," and a ritual gesture, saluting. When Antony, persuaded by the Roman's "style," announces his willingness to fight, Ventidius observes the transformation as a difference in speech and carriage which according to the rules of decorum define a new role for Antony to act:

> *Ant.* I warrant thee, old soldier.
> Thou shalt behold me once again in iron;
> And at the head of our old troops, that beat
> The Parthians, cry aloud—Come, follow me!
>
> *Vent.* Oh, now I hear my emperor! in that word
> Octavius fell....
>
> .   .   .   .
>
> Methinks, you breathe
> Another soul: Your looks are more divine;
> You speak a hero, and you move a god.   [I, i, p. 359]

Most often it is Antony who is the actor performing a part before the audience of other characters. This reading of the hero's nature Dryden may have borrowed from Shakespeare, whose Antony seems to lack an essential identity, who adopts styles he cannot reconcile, who is continually mocked by Cleopatra for performing roles he does not feel.[13] Yet Dryden's metaphor of Antony as an actor playing a series of parts has altogether different implications in the context of other expressive devices in *All for Love*. Dryden's Antony acknowledges his play-acting, but there is no suggestion that this is either a personal weakness or failure, or the calculated deception that Samson acts

out as defense in his final speeches.[14] Nor is it associated with Satanic "arts" of disguise or the pretenses
of an Achitophel. Furthermore, the other characters
who, like Ventidius, recognize his performances, do not
imply that such play-acting is a special flaw in Antony's nature or even a sign of his present surrender
to conflicting forces outside his control. On the contrary, they, like Ventidius, praise Antony when they
approve the manner of his acting, and continually ex-
hort him by titles that define his parts and therefore
dictate the appropriate words and gestures belonging
to the "style" of "Emperor," "Friend," "Husband,"
"Father," "Lover," "Soldier," "Roman," "Man." [15]
Frequently they define themselves by similar titles,
such as Octavia and Cleopatra exchange at their first
confrontation:

> *Octav.* I need not ask if you are Cleopatra;
> Your haughty carriage—
>
> *Cleo.* Shows I am a queen:
> Nor need I ask you, who you are.
>
> *Octav.* A Roman:
> A name, that makes and can unmake a queen.
>
> *Cleo.* Your lord, the man who serves me, is a Roman.
>
> *Octav.* He was a Roman, till he lost that name,
> To be a slave in Egypt . . .   [III, i, pp. 392-393]

Like Antony, they seem absorbed by "names" almost
as independent entities. As he confesses to have "dis-
graced/ The name of soldier" [I, i, p. 354] or accuses
Dolabella for profaning the "sacred name of friend"
[IV, i, p. 412], so Cleopatra speaks of her surrender
to Julius Cæsar as "due to the first name of men"

[II, i, p. 373] or attacks Octavia for holding the "specious title of a wife," while she herself must "bear the branded name of mistress" [III, i, p. 394].[16] Even at the very moment of her lover's death her feelings seem to be stirred by the authority of names:

I have not loved a Roman, not to know
What should become his wife; his wife, my Charmion!
For 'tis to that high title I aspire;
And now I'll not die less.   [V, i, pp. 432-433]

The quality of her actions is determined by the rules of "style" becoming to the roles of "Roman" and "wife." Whereas when Shakespeare's Cleopatra announces, "Husband, I come!/ Now to that name my courage prove my title!" [V, ii, 290-291], she claims her right by the authority of her own nature and acts, rather than by her knowledge of the rules of decorum, to which her "style" must be made to conform.

Dryden's metaphors for Antony's speeches as the repetition of lines in a play are therefore not signs of the hero's peculiar nature and situation, as are Shakespeare's in *Antony and Cleopatra,* so much as definitions of man's relationship to language. The other characters in *All for Love* also seem to recognize that they must be both actors and audience, must perform roles and interpret "styles" of speech. They therefore acknowledge the power of language and yet at the same time its essential meaninglessness. Implied in their attitude is the assumption that men are dependent on speech as their only medium of connection with one another. But because their choice of words is dictated by arbitrary rules of "style," their concern is for language independent of meanings. Ultimately they cannot judge the truth of words but only their effectiveness, whether they work as instruments, or persuade as an actor's delivery succeeds or fails to convince. The encounters between characters have a painfully empty sound, therefore, because they cannot consist of the exchange of inward experiences leading to communion, but only the utterance of finally meaningless sounds. The most extraordinary illustration of this attitude toward language is the last meeting between Antony and Cleopatra, which altogether misses the tragic force of Shakespeare's farewell scene, yet has its own oddly disturbing power:

> *Cleo.* 'Tis now too late
> To say I'm true: I'll prove it, and die with you.
> Unknown to me, Alexas feigned my death:
> Which, when I knew, I hastened to prevent
> This fatal consequence. My fleet betrayed
> Both you and me.
>
>   *Ant.* And Dolabella—
>
>   *Cleo.* Scarce
> Esteemed before he loved; but hated now.
>
>   *Ant.* Enough: my life's not long enough for more.
> Thou say'st, thou wilt come after: I believe thee;
> For I can now believe whate'er thou sayest,
> That we may part more kindly. [V, i, pp. 431-432]

That Antony's attention even in death should be given to words does not seem by now simply a failure of Dryden's to dramatize feelings, but evidence of attitudes repeatedly expressed in the play. Antony must talk about the words that Cleopatra uses and their effects upon him because language is the inevitable means of exchange even between lovers. Yet his speech is at the same time a painful admission of the irrelevance of words to feelings and therefore of the separateness of human beings who address each other with mutual acknowledgement that they are actors speaking according to prescribed "styles" rather than souls in communion. Antony's readiness, even at the moment of his death, to "believe whate'er" Cleopatra says follows the same formula of submission as his earlier surrenders to the hyperboles of Ventidius, the pleadings of Octavia and her supporters, the calculated rhetoric of Alexas. It expresses the same passivity and indifference. It is as if, like Samson, he renounces "talk" because it can bear no relation to "experience." Cleopatra's words seem to exert a transforming power over his feelings, not because they are charged with meanings at this moment of great emotional intensity, but because he recognizes and abandons himself to their arbitrariness. It does not matter whether or not they are true. Finally they are mere sounds, empty gestures, lines in a play. They are the only instruments by which the world may penetrate to the inward self, and yet the self remains forever separate.

In *All for Love,* as in *Samson Agonistes,* the experience of the hero is explored in images expressing the opposition of the self to the world that continually impinges on it by the power of language which is empty and irrelevant yet threatening. The destiny of the hero is his final escape from that world; his triumph is the achievement of inner inviolability as he passes beyond the reach of human utterance. This movement is expressed, although not always consistently, in Dryden's play by images of the hero's "retirement," "lethargy," "sleep," "oblivion," which parallel Samson's "separateness," "imprisonment," "impotence," "rest." These images for the hero's inward experience alter meanings in both works until each ends—Dryden's in some confusion—with a celebration of isolation, inactivity, and silence.

Antony's descriptions of his own experience at the beginning of *All for Love,* we have seen, resemble Samson's in their emphasis on his separateness and his impotence. He claims that he has been set apart from other men by a special destiny. Yet he also feels helpless in the power of forces outside himself, which exert their control even in his greatness, but above all in his defeat. The other characters, contrasting his present state with his former triumphs, in a manner similar to Samson's visitors, also find him peculiarly remote from life, inactive, impotent. Ventidius refers to Antony's "drooping spirits" [I, i, p. 347], a phrase that resembles a line from Samson's most terrible lament: "So much I feel my genial spirits droop" [594]. This mood drives Antony to retire not only from the world of public action but from all human society,[17] and we recall that Milton introduces Samson "Retiring" to an "unfrequented place" where he may express his sufferings only to himself. Antony's "retreat" is interpreted as the outward sign of "black despair" [I, i, p. 345], the spiritual condition of Samson in the opening lines of Milton's poem. He is in hiding from the world, in a kind of lethargy, as if he were asleep and "dreaming" (images suggested originally perhaps by Plutarch).[18] Or it is as if he had been transformed into some inhuman object—"The blank of what he was" [I, i, p. 349]—or some creature of nature. Ventidius, seeing him, like Samson as he first appears to the Chorus, abandoned in the traditional posture of despair, compares the hero to a stricken tree trunk:

How sorrow shakes him!
So, now the tempest tears him up by the roots,
And on the ground extends the noble ruin.

[I, i, p. 351]

In Antony's own fantasies, he disappears into a
landscape which, despite its pastoral details, is solitary
and grotesque. These images "lull" him as an escape
from men:

      . . . I fancy
I'm now turned wild, a commoner of nature;
Of all forsaken, and forsaking all;
Live in a shady forest's sylvan scene,
Stretched at my length beneath some blasted oak,
I lean my head upon the mossy bark,
And look just of a piece as I grew from it;
My uncombed locks, matted like mistletoe,
Hang o'er my hoary face; a murm'ring brook
Runs at my foot.

. . . .

    The herd come jumping by me.
And, fearless, quench their thirst, while I look on,
And take me for their fellow-citizen. [I, i, p. 351]

Dryden allows even Ventidius to feel some attraction
in these images of retirement and inertia, when he
can "fancy" himself as part of this landscape [I, i,
p. 351] or when he imagines Antony's death as restful
slumber—"Lie still and peaceful there" [I, i, p. 351].
These fantasies are, however, contradicted by the rest
of Ventidius' speeches here and throughout the play.
His position is otherwise consistent and clearly defined: behind his criticisms of Antony lies the whole
tradition of heroic values. To Ventidius this despairing

passivity is the dishonorable opposite of the heroic life
of action:

> . . . you sleep away your hours
> In desperate sloth, miscalled philosophy.
> Up, up, for honour's sake . . .   [I, i, p. 355]

Familiar with this traditional rhetoric, the audience
in the early scenes of the play is apparently asked to
share the Roman's judgment by responding to the
appeals of his heroic "style." We do so in part because
we ally ourselves with his cause against Alexas, but
more because Antony seems enfeebled and confused
in his desperate lethargy. We understand the images
of retirement, sleeping, inertia in the beginning of
All for Love to represent a spiritual collapse from
which the hero must recover, as Samson must in one
sense escape from his "Inseparably dark" imprisonment, if he is to triumph over his sufferings and
achieve his heroic goal.

When Antony, hearing of Cleopatra's supposed
death, finally renounces his "brave Roman fate"
[V, i, p. 424], Ventidius chides him again with "lethargy" and makes one last attempt to stir him with
rhetoric: "Come, rouse yourself, and let's die warm
together" [V, i, p. 427]. The scene follows the pattern
of their first encounter: the conflict is imagined in the
same terms. This time, however, Antony is unmoved
by appeals to his sense of honor (he plans to die "as
a Roman ought," but his given reasons are not those
of the code). His inertia now seems to represent a new
imperviousness to the power of eloquence, less fierce
than Samson's deafness to Dalila's persuasions, but
showing a change in him parallel to Samson's progress
"onward." Antony's speech displays a new resolute-

ness which gives a different meaning to his renunciation of the heroic "part" that Ventidius has always
urged him to perform:

> Yes, I would be taken;
> But, as a Roman ought,—dead, my Ventidius:
> For I'll convey my soul from Cæsar's reach,
> And lay down life myself. 'Tis time the world
> Should have a lord, and know whom to obey.
> We two have kept its homage in suspense,
> And bent the globe, on whose each side we trod,
> Till it was dented inwards. Let him walk
> Alone upon 't: I'm weary of my part.
> My torch is out; and the world stands before me,
> Like a black desert at the approach of night:
> I'll lay me down, and stray no farther on.
>
> [V, i, p. 428]

Antony's lines here do not sound as simply and
physically weary as those of Shakespeare's Antony:
"Unarm me, Eros. The long day's task is done,/ And
we must sleep" [IV, xiv, 35-36]. Dryden's hero gives a
political justification for his renunciation of the world
and argues a philosophical reason for his suicide.
Where Shakespeare's Antony with utmost simplicity
exposes how lost and weary he feels without Cleopatra
—"Since the torch is out,/ Lie down, and stray no
farther" [IV, xiv, 46-47]—Dryden transforms the
lines so that they express Antony's attitude toward
human life more than his feelings for Cleopatra. By
introducing the theatrical metaphor, Dryden directs
our attention to Antony's recognition of the emptiness
of performing parts, which is the way the play has
defined human society, public life, and even the most
intimate relationships. Following this metaphor, the

phrase "My torch is out" seems to refer less to Cleopatra (there is no ambiguity in Shakespeare's image, with its sexual suggestions of heat and flames) than to Antony himself. It is as if he has lost his lighted place in a procession or has moved to the boundary where civilization ends in deserted wilds, or perhaps more simply, has felt the quenching of his own vital heat. The image, with all its indefinite possibilities of interpretation, concentrates on Antony at the point of passage from one state to another, rather than on his immediate feelings of passionate loss. This emphasis is intensified in Dryden's version of Antony's death:

Cleo. Your words are like the notes of dying swans,
Too sweet to last. Were there so many hours
For your unkindness, and not one for love?

   Ant. No, not a minute.—This one kiss—more worth
Than all I leave to Cæsar.   [*Dies.*

   Cleo. O tell me so again,
And take ten thousand kisses for that word.
My lord, my lord! speak, if you yet have being;
Sign to me, if you cannot speak; or cast
One look! do anything that shows you live.

   Iras. He's gone too far to hear you;
And this you see, a lump of senseless clay,
The leavings of a soul.   [V, i, p. 432]

The motif of the final kiss (borrowed from Shakespeare) in Antony's last speech points to the theme of the play's main title: one embrace between lovers outweighs the whole world. But the emphasis of the scene, even the lines immediately following Antony's last words, prevent either a convincing affirmation of the triumph of love, such as we find in *Antony and Cleopatra,* or a condemnation of "unlawful" and enfeebling passion, such as we expect from Ventidius, the spokesman for heroic values, or such as Dryden seems to argue in the Preface to the play. The fullness of meaning here is rather in the description of Antony's escape from "being," the theme that of the play's subtitle, "The World Well Lost." Dying is for the hero the passage into the inertness of natural objects. A "lump of senseless clay" has none of the power of the things in nature to which Samson is finally compared, but it is equally impervious. Now Antony is truly the "blank of what he was." Like Samson in death, he has gone beyond the reach of words and therefore beyond the bounds of human society, beyond the appeals of honor and even the intimacy of love. His escape is a more passive version of Samson's violent negation of experience. It too ends in wordless unconsciousness, as if his own surmise is proved true: "death, for aught I know,/ Is but to think no more" [V, i, p. 430]. Iras' comment on this passage into oblivion makes a meaningful contrast with lines earlier in the play, in which Alexas advises Cleopatra how to charm Antony back to her:

Believe me, madam, Antony is yours.
His heart was never lost, but started off
To jealousy, love's last retreat and covert;
Where it lies hid in shades, watchful in silence,
And listening for the sound that calls it back.
[V, i, p. 419]

Now, Iras remarks, no sound, not even the eloquence of Cleopatra, can call Antony back to the world. In death his heart, or soul, or self is finally freed from his susceptibility to the power of language by achieving the imperviousness of things. The strongest impression made by his dying is the sense of his elusiveness as he escapes forever beyond recall to his "last retreat" of "shades" and "silence." He has achieved the oblivion for which Cleopatra earlier longed:

> For, if there be a place of long repose,
> I'm sure I want it. My disdainful lord
> Can never break that quiet; nor awake
> The sleeping soul, with holloing in my tomb
> Such words as fright her hence.   [IV, i, p. 402]

Here at Antony's death, as throughout the play, the most convincingly and consistently expressed view is of separateness rather than communion, so that when Cleopatra is made to describe her relationship to Antony in death as the recaptured privacy of passion —"We're now alone, in secrecy and silence;/ And is not this like lovers?" [V, i, p. 434]—we feel the irrelevance of this interpretation. What has been achieved is not intimacy between two human beings who set themselves against the world, for example like Donne's lovers in "The Canonization." What has been reached is closer to Samson's final attainment, the inviolability of the individual self.

This emphasis at the end of the play is increased by numerous images of dying and sleeping which Dryden borrowed from Shakespeare's final scenes (the original suggestion coming perhaps from Plutarch),[19] but which also recall the descriptions of Antony in retirement from the world at the beginning of *All for Love,* asleep and dreaming in his desperate lethargy. The sexual implications of the Shakespearean images are almost completely transformed in Dryden's version: the slumber of death is not sensual and passionate, but still and oblivious even for Cleopatra. To Shakespeare's Egyptian Queen:

> The stroke of death is as a lover's pinch,
> Which hurts, and is desir'd.   [V, ii, 298-299]

Dryden's Cleopatra welcomes death rather as an opiate than a lover. She greets the fatal aspic as a "deceiver" whose role is not sexual:

> Thou best of thieves; who, with an easy key,
> Dost open life, and, unperceived by us,
> Even steal us from ourselves; discharging so
> Death's dreadful office, better than himself;
> Touching our limbs so gently into slumber,
> That Death stands by, deceived by his own image,
> And thinks himself but sleep.   [V, i, p. 435]

The mood is altogether altered from the Shakespearean original, where Cleopatra in death represents passionate energy:

> . . . she looks like sleep,
> As she would catch another Antony
> In her strong toil of grace.   [V, ii, 349-351]

The parallel to these lines in Serapion's last speech lacks the vitality of Shakespeare's, and also the appropriateness, since the suggestion of a passionate union transcending death seems again irrelevant to Dryden's interpretation of the lovers' deaths elsewhere expressed. In Serapion's description:

> The impression of a smile, left in her face,
> Shows she died pleased with him for whom she lived,
> And went to charm him in another world.
>
> [V, i, p. 436]

Cleopatra's power to "charm" has been associated throughout the rest of the play with the threat of language wielded by her after the manner of the other characters, as she recites speeches whose "style" is arbitrarily dictated by the "title" or "name" she bears, the role she plays in the meaningless scheme of human relationships. Serapion's lines, therefore, though perhaps intended as a tribute to the transcendence of love, are actually contradicted elsewhere in the drama, as we have seen, and particularly by the images of sleeping and oblivion in the preceding death scenes.

By comparing the epitaphs spoken over the lovers as the closing lines of each play, we recognize how thoroughly Dryden has altered the significance of their dying, and how his changes suggest parallels with the end of *Samson Agonistes*. Both epitaphs, following the conventional formula, acknowledge in heroic language the magnitude of the protagonists' triumph even in death. In *Antony and Cleopatra* their achievement is passionate union transcending the world and time. Their tomb itself will embrace them, an image which, as it is spoken by the passionless Cæsar using the strangely earthy and literal verb "clip," pays tribute to the impressive power of their sexuality and their humanity:

> She shall be buried by her Antony.
> No grave upon the earth shall clip in it
> A pair so famous. High events as these

Strike those that make them; and their story is
No less in pity than his glory which
Brought them to be lamented. Our army shall
In solemn show attend this funeral,
And then to Rome. Come, Dolabella, see
High order in this great solemnity. [V, ii, 361-369]

The epitaph for Dryden's lovers unites them in
eternity, but their state is not imagined as the final
communion of souls in a heavenly marriage (although
there is an echo here of the narrator's address to
sleeping Adam and Eve in *P. L.,* IV, 773-774). They
are joined in the slumber of oblivion:

     Sleep, blest pair,
Secure from human chance, long ages out,
While all the storms of fate fly o'er your tomb . . .
                   [V, i, p. 436]

Their dying does not represent what Shakespeare's
Cleopatra claims to be the triumph of "Immortal
longings" [V, ii, 284] for union, as the earlier description of Cleopatra in Serapion's speech might intend
to suggest, nor the "unfortunate end" inevitable for
"crimes of love" in the traditional view of Ventidius
and of Dryden in the play's Preface. The language of
the final scenes actually presents the deaths of the
protagonists as the fulfillment of a desire which is
also antithetical to the urge toward power, the prize
to be gained through activity and energy by the
protagonists of Dryden's heroic dramas. The longing
satisfied for Antony and Cleopatra is the wish to
retreat from the world to the shelter, the safety, the
security of the grave. The "tomb" in which they
sleep shares the qualities of enclosure, protection, and

stillness with Samson's "fort of silence," though
without its suggestions of heroic defiance. The reward
of their greatness is the "rest" of inactivity, of
passivity, which makes them inviolate. They have
achieved the static condition belonging to souls in
Heaven as they are enviously envisioned by Adam at
the end of *The State of Innocence:*

> O goodness infinite! whose heavenly will
> Can so much good produce from so much ill!
> Happy their state!
> Pure, and unchanged, and needing no defence
> From sins, as did my frailer innocence.
> Their joy sincere, and with no sorrow mixed:
> Eternity stands permanent and fixed,
> And wheels no longer on the poles of time;
> Secure from fate, and more secure from crime.
>
> [V, i, pp. 176-177]

Both the play and the opera finally value a "perma-
nent and fixed" condition, "secure" from the accidents
of life and the vascillations of human feelings, from
time, change, "chance," "fate," "sin," "crime." This
condition of freedom suggests parallels with Samson's
liberation from the "mutable" ways of men. Dryden's
Antony and Cleopatra by their deaths are transformed
into a "state" which has still fewer suggestions of
immortal communion than the Heaven awaiting his
Adam and Eve; like Samson they have passed into
unconsciousness where even unmixed feelings cannot
reach them.

By escaping into oblivion, Dryden's lovers have
freed themselves at last from society, and we are
seemingly asked to value this release rather than
condemning it as a crime against duty and honor.

The manner in which they elude the world's hostile powers is not that of Shakespeare's Antony and Cleopatra, however. They have not through passion transcended the heroic code of honor and of public action by including it in the more expansive vision of Shakespeare's drama. They have cast heroism aside with the other weary roles the world has forced them to speak, and even love has been included among those roles, for throughout the play it has been subject to the same arbitrary, meaningless, and yet threatening limitations that define all human utterance and therefore human society. Their achievement is the denial of heroic public action—the "world" which Antony leaves to Cæsar— but also of the "silence and secrecy" of private passion, finally of all feeling, all experience.

Dryden's revisions of *Antony and Cleopatra,* his reshaping of dramatic form, his recasting of characters, his style—especially its devices learned apparently from the language of *Samson Agonistes*— tend to the presentation of this view of experience. The final scenes, for all their inconsistencies of attitude, mainly confirm such an interpretation, with the result that the conventional closing couplet sounds remarkably inappropriate to what the play chiefly expresses:

And fame to late posterity shall tell,
No lovers lived so great, or died so well.
[V, i, p. 436]

Its inappropriateness is not the irrelevance we hear in Manoa's traditional eulogy of Samson. That is, when Manoa speaks his praise for Samson's final act, which "heroicly hath finished/ A life Heroic" [1710-1711], the reader senses Manoa's meaning to be an inadequate interpretation of Samson's achievement but at the same time a dramatically right formulation for the limits of Manoa's understanding. Nor does the last couplet of Serapion's speech have the unexpected quality of Cæsar's epitaph for Shakespeare's lovers, which signifies that even the cold Roman is uncharacteristically moved by their heroic passion. The last lines of *All for Love* seem to be spoken rather perfunctorily by the poet, rather than the character, in the form of a conventional vow to immortalize the lives of great lovers.[20] Yet the traditional language of heroic poetry, as it is included among all human and social forms of utterance, has by implication in *All for Love* been denied the power to celebrate the triumph which the play mainly honors: the escape of the self into the security of silence. Like Samson when he fulfills his heroic destiny, Antony and Cleopatra have passed into a state "blest" because they can no longer hear whatever the world's representatives can "tell." *All for Love* therefore expresses attitudes close to those at the heart of *Samson Agonistes,* but the end of the play reduces them to confusion, for Dryden never follows the implications of this view of the morality of language to their extreme conclusions. Adopting the Roman formula of a conventional Shakespearean epitaph,[21] Dryden in his final couplet returns as though with full affirmation to traditional values—a celebration of heroic action, honor, love, fame, poetry—which *All for Love* has chiefly renounced as the empty "styles" of a world well lost.

Conclusion: Literary Traditions

The consciously elaborated pattern of connections between *Absalom and Achitophel* and *Paradise Lost* associates Dryden as a poet with his older contemporary, as Milton's richly various absorptions of traditional materials into the language of his epic place him in living association with poets of earlier times. Both works present a view of our vicious and fragmented world where morality has been reduced to verbal chaos, both using a language which by contrast recreates ideal images from the past. Milton locates the source of these images in Eden; Dryden (for whom an original state of innocence had the quality of a metaphor rather than a fact) finds them in Milton's epic and its literary heritage. By evoking these ideal images in language which continually relates itself to other works of literature, both writers assert the unique power of the poet's eloquence as a force for the restoration of order in human experience. They claim moral authority by the special poetic character of their utterances, and because the efficacy of their language depends in large part upon the reader's shared ability to recognize and respond to their connections with literary tradition, their claim depends upon a sense of poetry as communion. The exertion of the poet's gift is a social (or "sociable") as well as a moral act: his special eloquence teaches individual men their proper relation to larger orders of human experience in society. These are the attitudes of Milton in *Paradise Lost* and Dryden in *Absalom and Achitophel*. They represent a point of view inherited from writers of earlier times whose ideals were preserved in literature. These works are firmly rooted in a continuing tradition linking them with classical, Renaissance and earlier seventeenth-century poetry and making possible the rich poetic assimilations of Pope.

For all their fullness and assurance, however, these traditional attitudes were never finally fixed for either Milton or Dryden; neither poet held to them with the consistency of Sidney or Jonson before them, or of Pope, their great successor. Dryden's uncertainty in this position is suggested by the grandiose emptiness of his early attempts at heroic poetry, by his distrust of pastoral idealizing, in the ethical confusions of his heroic dramas, and more particularly by the contradictions of attitude at the end of *Absalom and Achitophel* and in *All for Love*. Milton's diversion from this tradition is fully expressed in only one of his major works, *Samson Agonistes*, but with such conviction and in such extreme terms that we recognize it to be deeply felt. Dryden himself must have responded to the force of that expression, for in *All for Love*, despite its confusions, he drew near to the peculiar vision of Milton's dramatic poem. He created in Antony an image of man's inward self whose isolation and final escape from the world of men is presented in a style that, by its most curious patterns of expression, exposes the emptiness of all human forms of utterance and therefore the impossibility of personal, social, or literary communion.

In *Samson Agonistes* Milton may be said again to contrast the fallen ways of men in society with ideal images, but their source is altogether outside human history, in a timeless and immutable world, and their efficacy is restored not by eloquence but by silence. The style of the poem seems designed, therefore, not to accumulate the fullest resources of language, like the poetry of *Paradise Lost,* but to escape its restrictions and the bounds of human experience. In the dramatic poem, then, Milton asserts perhaps even prouder authority for poetry than the traditional power of eloquence urged in the epic. Yet his claims are paradoxical, denying literature its role as a social force for morality, while asserting greater gifts for the inward powers which can transcend human limits— represented by the language of men—to a vision of eternal silence. This vision, to which Dryden was strongly attracted, is a prediction, not of Pope's achievements, but of Wordsworth's.

Such profound lack of consistency in the attitudes of the two greatest poets of the later seventeenth century shows the difficulty of defining this period of English literature. The evidence that Dryden and Milton, for all their differences in religious and political affiliations, in social and literary interests, shared this radical division of attitudes, points to such lack of consistency itself as a defining characteristic of poetry in this phase of literary history. Without giving in to the temptation of facilely naming causes, we might think of the period as one in which a rich literary heritage was still widely and easily familiar, making possible between the poet and his definable audience a communion of shared associations and analogies that related their experiences to traditional ideals. This inheritance Milton and Dryden transmitted to Pope. We might also think of the seventeenth century as a time sharply divided in the minds of Englishmen by changes so violent that they seemed to separate the later decades from earlier history as a distinction between two worlds. In this view, even poets of the preceding generation, as well as the "ancients," wrote a language which seemingly demanded translation to be understood by Englishmen of the next age. This need implied a sense of alienation from old feelings, attitudes, values, as well as a rejection of antiquated style, since to these poets language and morality inevitably define each other. When Milton and Dryden deviated, therefore, from older points of view, or altered earlier literary models, they showed some sense of the inadequacy or irrelevance or inaccessibility of traditional ideals—classical and Christian, continental and English—to their interpretation of experience. They tried out uses of language which predicted a new direction for English literature, new claims for the poet's powers, new connections with literary tradition, ultimately finding expression by Wordsworth. In the conflict between these literary strains, the two greatest poets of the later seventeenth century explored the morality of language.

Introduction: Literary Connections

1. Mark Van Doren, *John Dryden* (Bloomington, 1960), p. 103: "Milton's impact upon Dryden was not sudden, nor was his influence of a permeating kind. The two poets were worlds apart."

2. See W. R. Parker, *Milton's Contemporary Reputation* (Columbus, 1940); Morris Freedman, "Dryden's Reported Reaction to *Paradise Lost*," *NQ*, CCIII (January 1958), 14-16; M. Manuel, *The Seventeenth Century Critics and Biographers of Milton* (Kerala, 1962). It is generally agreed that work on *Paradise Lost* was begun before 1660 and that *Samson Agonistes* was written after the epic. For arguments challenging this order see for example Alan Gilbert, "Is *Samson Agonistes* Unfinished?" *PQ*, XXVIII (January 1949), 98-106; W. R. Parker, "The Date of *Samson Agonistes*," *PQ*, XXVIII (January 1949), 145-166.

3. "An Essay of Dramatic Poesy," *Essays of John Dryden*, ed. W. P. Ker (New York: Russell and Russell, 1961), I, 35. Quotations from Dryden's essays are taken from this edition whenever possible. Those not included by Ker are taken from *The Works of John Dryden*, ed. Sir Walter Scott, rev. George Saintsbury (London: William Patterson, 1882-1893).

4. Dryden suggests this notion in the Prologue to *Aureng-Zebe:* "Let him retire, betwixt two Ages cast,/The first of this, and hindmost of the last" [21-22]. All quotations from Dryden's non-dramatic poetry are taken from *The Poems and Fables of John Dryden*, ed. James Kinsley (London: Oxford University Press, 1962). References are given to line numbers for the poetry, to page numbers for prefatory remarks in prose.

5. "The Reason of Church Government Urged Against Prelaty," *The Student's Milton*, ed. F. A. Patterson (New York: F. S. Crofts, 1947), pp. 524, 526. All quotations from Milton's writings are taken from this edition; references are given to line numbers for the poetry and to page numbers for the prose.

6. The suggestion in *Paradise Lost*, VII, 31, that the poet expects to find only "fit audience . . . though few" is contradicted by his large intention to "justifie the wayes of God to men" [I, 26] and by the vastness and inclusiveness of the epic itself, which tells the story of the "whole included Race" [IX, 416].

7. "The Verse," *Student's Milton*, p. 159. The preface as a contribution to the controversy between Dryden and Sir Robert Howard on rhyme is discussed by David Masson, *The Life of John Milton* (London, 1880), VI, 633-634; Morris Freedman, "Milton and Dryden on Rhyme," *HLQ*, XXIV (August 1961), 337-344.

8. "On *Paradise Lost*," *Student's Milton*, pp. 158-159. Milton's "old fashioned" blank verse is again the subject of comments in the pamphlet controversy between Marvell and Samuel Parker. See Masson, *Life of Milton*, VI, 704-709.

9. *The State of Innocence* was not printed until three years after Marvell's poem, but Dryden, in "The Author's Apology for Heroic Poetry and Poetic License" prefixed to the published opera, gives as his reason for that edition the fact that "many hundred copies" full of errors had been "dispersed abroad without my knowledge or consent . . ." *Essays*, I, 178.

10. The pseudonym "Bayes," referring to Dryden's position as poet-laureate, was used in Buckingham's *Rehearsal* (1672).

11. "To Mr. Dryden, On His Poem of Paradise," *Works*, V, 109.

12. The suggestion is supported by some remarks in Dryden's essays, for example "Preface to *Sylvæ*," *Essays*, I, 268: "Cannot I admire the height of his [Milton's] invention, and the strength of his expression, without defending his antiquated words, and the perpetual harshness of their sound?" See also: "A Discourse Concerning the Original and Progress of Satire," *Essays*, II, 29, 109; George Williamson, "Dryden's View of Milton," *Milton and Others* (London, 1965), pp. 102-121.

13. "To the Unknown Author of This Excellent Poem," *Works*, IX, 215.

14. See for example Samuel Johnson, "Life of Pope," *Lives of the English Poets* (London, 1961), II, 306: "He professed to have learned his poetry from Dryden, whom, whenever an opportunity was presented, he praised through his whole life with unvaried liberality . . ."; p. 326: "By perusing the works of Dryden, he discovered the most perfect fabrick of English verse, and habituated himself to that only which he found the best . . ." The great exception to this view is F. R. Leavis, "The Line of Wit," *Revaluation* (London, 1936), pp. 10-41.

15. Reuben Brower, "Dryden and the 'Invention' of Pope," *Restoration and Eighteenth-Century Literature*, ed. Carroll Camden (Chicago, 1963), p. 211.

16. Brower, "Dryden and the 'Invention' of Pope," p. 211. In "An Allusion to Europe: Dryden and the Poetic Tradition," *Alexander Pope* (Oxford, 1959), pp. 1-14, Mr. Brower stresses Dryden's position as precursor of Pope, but throughout the rest of the book he makes his readers also aware of Pope's indebtedness to Milton.

17. Since *Absalom and Achitophel*, Part I, was conceived and composed as a separate poem, mentions of that title in this book refer only to Part I. The second part, published a year later, was written largely by Tate, although Dryden contributed some lines.

18. In the Preface to *All for Love*, *Essays*, I, 201, Dryden hopes that by "imitating" Shakespeare "I have excelled myself throughout the play . . ." In 1695, in "A Parallel of Poetry and Painting," *Essays*, II, 152, he claims the play to be the only one he wrote "for myself."

19. Van Doren, *John Dryden*, pp. 103-105 points out echoes of the "Ode on the Morning of Christ's Nativity" in "Heroique Stanzas" (137-140), of "Lycidas" and *Areopagitica* in "Annus Mirabilis" (925-927, 1169-1170) as well as echoes of *Samson Agonistes* in *Aureng-Zebe* and *Œdipus*, discussed elsewhere in this book. Borrowings from *Paradise Lost* in *Tyrannic Love* have been pointed out, for example by Charles Ward, *The Life of John Dryden* (Chapel Hill, 1961), pp. 70-75.

20. See "Lines on Milton" prefixed to the Fourth Edition of *Paradise Lost* in 1688. In "The Author's Apology for Heroic Poetry," prefixed to *The State of Innocence*, he calls *Paradise Lost* "undoubtedly one of the greatest, most noble, and most sublime poems which either this age or nation has produced" (*Essays*, I, 179).

21. Connections between the two works have often been noticed and discussed, although their variety and implications have not been fully

explored. See for example: Morris Freedman, ''Dryden's Miniature Epic,'' *JEGP*, LVII (April 1958), 211-219, and ''Satan and Shaftesbury,'' *PMLA*, LXXIV (December 1959), 544-547; Bernard Schilling, *Dryden and the Conservative Myth* (New Haven, 1961), pp. 195-199; Ruth Wallerstein, ''To Madness Near Allied,'' *HLQ*, VI (August 1943), 445-471.

22. T. S. Eliot contributed to the traditional separation of Milton and Dryden even by his conjunction of them as villains and victims of the ''dissociation of sensibility'' by emphasizing the different ways in which they influenced English poetry. See ''The Metaphysical Poets,'' *Selected Essays* (New York, 1932), pp. 247-250; ''John Dryden,'' pp. 264-274; ''Milton I,'' *On Poetry and Poets* (New York, 1957), pp. 156-164. Against this view E. M. W. Tillyard argues in *Poetry Direct and Oblique* (London, 1934), pp. 81-82 that the two poets shared a number of qualities including ''magniloquence.''

23. Dryden says, for example, of Shakespeare's language in the Preface to *Troilus and Cressida*, *Essays*, I, 203: ''Yet it must be allowed to the present age, that the tongue in general is so much refined since Shakespeare's time, that many of his words, and more of his phrases, are scarce intelligible. And of those which we understand, some are ungrammatical, others coarse; and his whole style is so pestered with figurative expressions, that it is as affected as it is obscure. 'Tis true, that in his latter plays he had worn off somewhat of the rust; but the tragedy which I have undertaken to correct was in all probability one of his first endeavours on the stage.''

24. These borrowings are listed by Edward LeComte, ''*Samson Agonistes* and *Aureng-Zebe*,'' *Etudes Anglaises*, XI (January 1958), 18-22. For discussion of the passage in *Œdipus* see Part II, chap. 1.

25. Some resemblances between the plays are noted, in altogether different terms from those of this book, by Morris Freedman, '' 'All for Love' and 'Samson Agonistes,' '' *NQ*, CCI (December 1956), 514-517.

26. For such a view, see for example George Wasserman, *John Dryden* (New York, 1964), p. 151: ''. . . it may seem rather faint praise to celebrate Dryden in the name of an age which is synonymous with artistic restraint and intellectual commitment and acceptance. Dryden was committed to the assumptions of Neoclassicism—to monarchy, to the couplet, to the lofty ideals of the heroic and the sublime; what distinguishes him from all but the greatest of his literary descendants was his ability to function freely within those assumptions. 'Luckily for himself, his age, and the history of English poetry,' writes Bernard Schilling, 'he was free though committed, at ease in conformity—able therefore, to do as he pleased.' ''

27. For an example of this opinion, see Douglas Bush, *English Literature in the Earlier Seventeenth Century*, 2nd ed. (Oxford, 1962), p. 378: Milton is seen ''as the last great exponent of Christian humanism in its historical continuity, the tradition of classical reason and culture fused with Christian faith which had been the main line of European development; his beliefs and attitudes, intensified and somewhat altered by the conditions of his age and country and by his own temperament, became as he grew old a noble anachronism in an alien world.''

28. ''Essay of Dramatic Poesy,'' *Essays*, I, 56.

PART ONE
I. Poetic Contexts: Parody, Imitation, Allusion

1. *The State of Innocence* was adapted for performance as a puppet show at Martin Powell's Punch Theatre in Covent Garden in 1712. See Hugh MacDonald, *John Dryden: A Bibliography* (Oxford, 1939), p. 115.

2. "The State of Innocence," *Works*, V, ed. Scott-Saintsbury, I, ii, p. 140. All quotations from Dryden's dramatic works are taken from this edition, in which lines are not numbered. References are therefore given to act, scene and page numbers.

3. It can be argued that with regard to certain theological and philosophical questions Dryden was quite deliberately revising Milton's attitudes. See Bruce King, "The Significance of Dryden's *State of Innocence*," *Studies in English Literature*, IV (Summer 1964), 371-391; A. W. Verrall, *Lectures on Dryden* (Cambridge, 1914), p. 225. Dryden in the "Author's Apology," *Essays*, I, 178, claims that the opera was written in a month "and not since revised."

4. Dryden's technical experiments in reworking *Paradise Lost* are discussed by George McFadden, "Dryden's 'Most Barren Period'—and Milton," *HLQ*, XXIV (August 1961), 283-296.

5. "To the Reader," *Poems*, p. 189: "*But, since the most excellent Natures are always the most easy; and, as being such, are the soonest perverted by ill Counsels, especially when baited with Fame and Glory; 'tis no more a wonder that he withstood not the temptations of Achitophel, than it was for Adam, not to have resisted the two Devils; the Serpent, and the Woman.*" See *P.L.*, IV, 302, 490; V, 352; VIII, 221-223. Echoes of Dante and Chaucer in line 30 are noted by James Kinsley, ed., *The Poems of John Dryden* (Oxford, 1958), IV, 1880.

6. *I Henry IV*, III, ii. All references to Shakespeare's plays are based on the edition of G. L. Kittredge, *The Complete Works of Shakespeare* (Boston: Ginn and Co., 1936).

7. Dryden's allusion is to the description of Satan with which Milton begins *P.L.*, II.

8. Dryden uses the word "damn" in this sense with great frequency in his Prologues and Epilogues. See especially: Prologue to *The Maiden Queen*; Epilogue to *Tyrannic Love*; Prologue to *The Assignation*; Prologue to *Œdipus*; Epilogue to *Troilus and Cressida*.

9. This identification is challenged and the name of Arthur Capel, Earl of Essex, is suggested as an alternative by James Kinsley, "Historical Allusions in *Absalom and Achitophel*," *RES*, VI, n.s. (July 1955), 293-294.

10. To Scott's explanation of the historical episode, the relevant Biblical allusion to Leviticus x:1 is added by George Noyes, ed., *The Poetical Works of John Dryden* (Cambridge, 1950), p. 961.

11. The relevant Biblical passage is Judges xix:22-25. The use of the label "Sons of Belial" by Puritan pamphleteers in attacks on dissolute Cavaliers is discussed by George Whiting, *Milton's Literary Milieu* (Chapel Hill, 1939), pp. 222-231. Dryden's line may also refer to the familiar use of the phrase as a pun referring to members of Balliol College, which was the Whig headquarters during the Oxford

Parliament, according to Hugh Cunningham, ''Sons of Belial,'' *TLS*, (June 10, 1939).

12. See Reuben Brower, ''Dryden's Epic Manner and Virgil,'' *PMLA*, LV (March 1940) 132-134.

13. The tradition which made the Old Testament figure of Achitophel [II Samuel xiii-xvi] into a commonplace type of the false politician is discussed by Richard F. Jones, ''The Originality of *Absalom and Achitophel*,'' *MLN*, XLVI (April 1931), 211-218. See also Howard Schless, ''Dryden's *Absalom and Achitophel* and *A Dialogue Between Nathan and Absalome*,'' *PQ*, XL (January 1961), 139-143. Dryden likens Achitophel-Shaftesbury to Satan again in ''The Medall,'' especially in lines 20-21, 30-31, 257-266, but the comparison is less extensive and is not included in a larger analogy with Milton's epic.

14. Borrowings in this passage have been identified from such a variety of writers as Spenser, Thomas Fuller, Thomas Carew, Robert Burton, Aristotle, Plato, Seneca, Hobbes, the Earl of Mulgrave.

15. For discussion of Milton's use of the word ''all'' see William Empson, *The Structure of Complex Words* (Norfolk, Conn., n.d.), pp. 101-104.

16. Lines 156-157 may literally refer to a real wound and drainage tube in Shaftesbury's side, according to Bruce King, ''Dryden's *Absalom and Achitophel*, 150-166,'' *Explicator*, XXI (December 1962).

17. The resemblance of Milton's Sin and Death to Spenserian allegory, especially to the description of Errour in *The Faerie Queene*, Book I, Canto i, has often been noticed. For discussion of Milton's parodic use of Spenser's and other styles see Anne D. Ferry, *Milton's Epic Voice* (Cambridge, Mass., 1963), pp. 122-133.

18. Here and throughout the discussion of this passage I am greatly indebted to William Youngren, ''Generality in Augustan Satire,'' *In Defense of Reading*, ed. Reuben Brower and Richard Poirier (New York, 1963), pp. 206-234.

19. Inspired by Satan, Eve dreams of flying in *P.L.*, V, 86-90; Sin echoes these lines after man's Fall [X, 243-244]; Adam and Eve, having eaten, feel ''Divinitie within them breeding wings/ Wherewith to scorn the Earth'' [IX, 1010-1011] and ''Bold'' is Adam's adjective for Eve's adventure [IX, 921].

II. *Satanic Rhetoric*

1. *P.L.*, I, 13, 16; IX, 20, 24.

2. See Ferry, *Milton's Epic Voice*, pp. 119-146. When T. S. Eliot in his attack on Milton described one of Satan's speeches as ''*rhetoric*'' in ''Milton I,'' p. 161, he failed to understand that this is precisely its intended effect, that this is Satan's style as distinct from the poet's.

3. For a reading of these speeches see M. M. Mahood, *Poetry and Humanism* (New Haven, 1950), pp. 215-216. The importance of titles in ''demonic oratory'' is discussed by John Steadman, '' 'Magnific Titles': Satan's Rhetoric and the Argument of Nobility,'' *MLR*, LXI (October 1966), 561-571.

4. Answering Abdiel, Satan claims to be ''self-begot, self-rais'd'' [V, 860], in contrast to Adam, whose first thoughts prove the existence of ''some great Maker'' [VIII, 278].

5. For Milton's stirring use of ennobling titles see for example "Areopagitica," *Student's Milton*, pp. 732, 753. Milton not only uses sarcasm habitually against his adversaries, but frequently makes explicit defense of such modes. For one example, see "An Apology for Smectymnuus," *Student's Milton*, p. 552: "'If therefore the question were in oratory, whether a vehement vein throwing out indignation or scorn upon an object that merits it, were among the aptest *ideas* of speech to be allowed, it were my work, and that an easy one, to make it clear both by the rules of best rhetoricians, and the famousest examples of the Greek and Roman orations. But since the religion of it is disputed, and not the art, I shall make use only of such reasons and authorities as religion cannot except against . . . Our Saviour, who had all gifts in him, was Lord to express his indoctrinating power in what sort him best seemed; sometimes by a mild and familiar converse; sometimes with plain and impartial home-speaking, regardless of those whom the auditors might think he should have had in more respect; otherwhiles, with bitter and ireful rebukes, if not teaching, yet leaving excuseless those his wilful impugners.' "

6. See also *P.L.*, IX, 137. Similarly Beelzebub, who consistently speaks for Satan, using his rhetoric, reveals the same theory of language:

> Thrones and imperial Powers, off-spring of heav'n,
> Ethereal Vertues; or these Titles now
> Must we renounce, and changing stile be call'd
> Princes of Hell? . . .   [II, 310-313]

7. This allusion to *Iliad*, XVI, 745-750 is pointed out by M. Y. Hughes, ed., *Paradise Lost* (New York, 1935), p. 204n.

8. Satan's speeches as a parody of classical orators and an allusion to Plato's sophists are discussed by John Steadman, "Image and Idol: Satan and the Element of Illusion in *Paradise Lost*," *JEGP*, LIX (October 1960), 640-654. For some other discussions of parody, burlesque and irony in Satan's speeches see: C. S. Lewis, *A Preface to Paradise Lost* (London, 1954), pp. 92-100; Arnold Stein, *Answerable Style* (Minneapolis, 1953), pp. 3-37; Joseph Summers, *The Muse's Method* (Cambridge, Mass., 1962), pp. 32-70; Charles Williams, ed., *The English Poems of John Milton* (London, 1940), introd.

9. Writing of "Annus Mirabilis," Dryden uses "elocution" to mean conscious art in the epistle prefixed to the poem, the "Letter to the Honorable, Sir Robert Howard," *Poems*, p. 46: ". . . *as I have endeavour'd to adorn it with noble thoughts, so much more to express those thoughts with elocution.*"

10. Milton himself makes explicit the parallels between Satan's temptations of Eve and Christ in *Paradise Regained*, IV, 1-6:

> Perplex'd and troubl'd at his bad success
> The Tempter stood, nor had what to reply,
> Discover'd in his fraud, thrown from his hope,
> So oft, and the perswasive Rhetoric
> That sleek't his tongue, and won so much on *Eve*,
> So little here, nay lost . . .

For other examples see *P.R.*, II, 140-143, 348-349; IV, 179-180. For one of the fullest discussions of Dryden's uses of *Paradise Regained* in *Absalom and Achitophel*, especially for Achitophel's Satanic portrait and Absalom's ironic Christhood, see A. B. Chambers, "Absalom and Achitophel: Christ and Satan," *MLN*, LXXIV (November 1959), 592-596.

11. The echoes are very loud in this speech of Satan's tempting of Christ in *Paradise Regained*, especially Book III, 21-42. The reader is perhaps also intended to recall the appeals made to Achilles in *Iliad*, Book IX, as well as the advice of Henry IV to Prince Hal in *I Henry IV*, III, ii.

12. For some examples see *Leviathan*, ed. Herbert Schneider (New York, 1958): "Imagination, therefore, is nothing but *decaying sense*" (p. 27); "All other names are but insignificant sounds" (p. 43); "For Reason, in this sense, is nothing but *reckoning* (p. 46). For discussion of Hobbes and Dryden see for example Louis Bredvold, *The Intellectual Milieu of John Dryden* (Ann Arbor, 1956).

13. G. M. Trevelyan, *England Under the Stuarts*, 20th ed. (London, 1947), p. 308, dates Charles' secret Catholicism as early as 1669, but the incredulous tone of Dryden's narrator (in "the King himself") suggests that the poet either was ignorant of the fact or here at least pretended ignorance.

III. The "Alter'd Stile" of Fallen Men

1. This metaphor is noticed by J. B. Broadbent, *Some Graver Subject* (New York, 1960), p. 249; A. B. Giamatti, *The Earthly Paradise and the Renaissance Epic* (Princeton, 1966), p. 342.

2. This allusion to the *Iliad*, III, 441-446 is discussed by Douglas Bush, *Paradise Lost in Our Time* (Ithaca, N. Y., 1945), p. 105.

3. The echo in this passage of Odysseus' speech to Agamemnon in the *Iliad*, XIV, 83 is noted by Hughes, ed., *Paradise Lost*, p. 310n.

4. Eve's equation of "imputing" with willfullness is measured against God's pronouncement of the doctrine of "imputed righteousness" granted to man by Christ's sacrifice [III, 291]. See also "The Christian Doctrine," *Student's Milton*, p. 1017.

5. According to Noyes, ed., *Works*, p. 959: "*Patriot* was the name affected by the faction (the germ of the Whig party) that in 1680 sent up petitions to Charles asking him to allow Parliament to meet, that the Exclusion Bill might be passed."

6. For such flippant use of "cursed" see for example the second Prologue to *The Maiden Queen*.

7. These implications are discussed by Christopher Ricks, "Dryden's Absalom," *Essays in Criticism*, XI (July 1961), 273-289.

8. The resemblance between these lines and the opening couplet of Dryden's translation of "The Sixth Satire of Juvenal" is mentioned by Ian Jack, *Augustan Satire* (Oxford, 1961), pp. 74-75. Their resemblance to Donne's *Elegies*, xvii, 38-49 is noted by Kingsley, *Poems*, IV, 1879. A number of Dryden's notions discussed here are also traditional to "libertine" pastoral; for an English example see "A Rapture," *The Poems of Thomas Carew*, ed. R. Dunlap (Oxford, 1949), pp. 49-53.

9. Dryden's imagery of floods, disease, and lunacy recalls Michael's presentation to Adam of the consequences of sin in *P.L.*, XI, 471-490, 738-753.

10. *Leviathan*, Part I, Chapter 13.

11. See Prologue to *The Unhappy Favorite*:

> Our Land's an *Eden*, and the Main's our Fence,
> While we Preserve our State of Innocence;
> That lost, then Beasts their Brutal Force employ,
> And first their Lord, and then themselves destroy:
> What Civil Broils have cost we know too well,
> Oh let it be enough that once we fell,
> And every Heart conspire with every Tongue,
> Still to have such a King, and this King Long.   [27-34]

For discussion of Dryden's use of the "matter of Eden" see Alan Roper, *Dryden's Poetic Kingdoms* (London, 1965), pp. 104-135.

12. Dryden argues the usefulness of history in "The Life of Plutarch," *Works*, XVII, 56: "For mankind being the same in all ages, agitated by the same passions, and moved to action by the same interests, nothing can come to pass, but some precedent of the like nature has already been produced; so that having the causes before our eyes, we cannot easily be deceived in the effects, if we have judgment enough but to draw the parallel." This passage is discussed by R. E. Hughes, "John Dryden's Greatest Compromise," *Studies in Literature and Language*, II (Winter 1961), 458-463.

13. For example see "To my Honour'd Friend, Dr. Charleton" (11-14) or the Prologue to *The Indian Queen*. The pastoral idea is most characteristically associated for Dryden with retirement from London life, as in the Epilogue to the University of Oxford, 1674 (1-6). In the accompanying Prologue, pastoral language is used for burlesque (3-8).

14. For example "Astraea Redux" (292-293) and "Annus Mirabilis" (71) allude to the same lines from Virgil's Fourth Eclogue (5-8) that are echoed in the last lines of *Absalom and Achitophel*.

15. See especially Act I, scene ii; Act II, scene ii.

IV. The Restorative Power of Eloquence

1. Following the formula of Genesis itself, Raphael catalogues the works of the six days as the creation of both things and their names: "God said, let ther be Firmament . . ./ and God made/ The Firmament/ . . . And Heav'n he nam'd the Firmament" [VII, 261, 263-264, 274].

2. Milton chose to add these lines in a prominent position to make a suitable introduction for Book VIII when, in the second edition of 1674, he redivided the epic into twelve books instead of the original ten. Adam playfully attributes magical power to Raphael's "potent voice" when he imagines that the sun will delay its course to hear the angel's story [VII, 99-101]. The "Charming" power of Raphael's speech is a contrast to the "pleasing sorcerie" of "Eloquence" in Hell [II, 556-566]. For discussion of this passage and of Satanic eloquence see Dennis

Burden, *The Logical Epic* (Cambridge, Mass., 1967), pp. 58-60, 130, 141-143.

3. Dryden remarks in "Original and Progress of Satire," *Essays,* II, 44: "After God had cursed Adam and Eve in Paradise, the husband and wife excused themselves, by laying the blame on one another; and gave a beginning to those conjugal dialogues in prose, which the poets have perfected in verse."

4. Dryden's preoccupation with the state of nature imagined as a combination of Hobbes' theory and Milton's descriptions is shown in the ending he gives to *The State of Innocence,* V, i, pp. 177-178:

> *Raph.* The rising winds urge the tempestuous air;
> And on their wings deformed winter bear:
> The beasts already feel the change; and hence
> They fly to deeper coverts, for defence:
> The feebler herd before the stronger run;
> For now the war of nature is begun:
> But, part you hence in peace, and having mourned your sin,
> For outward Eden lost, find Paradise within.

5. This important point needs no further elaboration here, because the redemptive function of Eve's speech as an echo of Christ's, and its place in the larger structural patterns of the poem, is analysed in detail by Summers, *The Muse's Method,* pp. 176-185. For discussion of relevant theological questions see Jackson Boswell, "Milton and Prevenient Grace," *Studies in English Literature,* VII (Winter 1967), 83-94.

6. The transformation of "evensong" into confession is noted by Broadbent, *Some Graver Subject,* p. 266.

7. In the view of Stein, *Answerable Style,* p. 117: "Before the Fall the highest value is knowledge . . . After the Fall the highest value is love." For comments on the "advantage in moral and spiritual qualities" given to Eve see: Helen Gardner, *A Reading of Paradise Lost* (Oxford, 1965), pp. 87-88; Irene Samuel, *Dante and Milton* (Ithaca, N. Y., 1966), pp. 243-244.

8. Stein, *Answerable Style,* pp. 75-118. See also Ferry, *Milton's Epic Voice,* pp. 108-111.

9. See for example "The Christian Doctrine," *Student's Milton,* p. 999: "It cannot be denied, however, that some remnants of the divine image still exist in us, not wholly extinguished by this spiritual death."

10. "Of Education," *Student's Milton,* p. 729: To the study of logic and rhetoric "poetry would be made subsequent, or indeed rather precedent, as being less subtile and fine, but more simple, sensuous, and passionate." The purpose of such study would be to show "what religious, what glorious and magnificent use might be made of poetry, both in, divine and human things." Milton's notion of the uses of poetry in the fallen world is significantly close to that of Sir Philip Sidney in his *Defense of Poesy.* For discussion of Milton's theory see Frank Kermode, "Adam Unparadised," *The Living Milton* (London, 1960), pp. 91-94.

11. These assertions are found especially in the opening invocation [I, 1-26] and in the invocation announcing the end to communion between man and God or angels [IX, 1-47].

12. See *Iliad*, I, 530; *Aeneid*, IX, 106. In *The State of Innocence* this formula marks the creation of man [I, i, p. 130] and also the consummation of Adam's marriage [III, i, p. 143]. The use of this convention for parody in "MacFlecknoe" and to dignify in the later satire is discussed by Albert Ball, "Charles II: Dryden's Christian Hero," *MP*, LIX (August 1961), 25-35. Milton's God speaks again in thunder when he announces man's Fall to the heavenly host [X, 33].

13. Samuel Johnson, despite his royalist sympathies, recognized the confusion at the end of the satire. He says of the King's speech and its predicted effect, in "Life of Dryden," *Lives*, I, 309: "Who can forbear to think of an enchanted castle, with a wide moat and lofty battlements, walls of marble and gates of brass, which vanishes at once into air, when the destined knight blows his horn before it?" The confusion cannot be explained away by the observation that David's speech is a "reflection of the Last Judgment," as is argued by Barbara Lewalski, "The Scope and Function of Biblical Allusion in *Absalom and Achitophel*," *ELN*, III (September 1965), 34. For discussion of the historical background of the King's speech see Godfrey Davies, "The Conclusion of Dryden's *Absalom and Achitophel*," *HLQ*, X (November 1946), 69-82.

14. The word "pious" is used in this sense by the King in line 983.

15. *P.L.*, VIII, 429, 418; IV, 689; IX, 1, 237; IV, 639; IX, 909. Eden as a "society," but one particularly resembling England prior to the seventeenth century, is argued by Jeffrey Hart, "*Paradise Lost* and Order," *CE*, XXV (May 1964), 576-582.

16. *The Faerie Queene*, Book I, Canto X, Stanza 56: the angels "with great joy into that Citie wend,/ As commonly as friend does with his frend." References to Raphael's "Sociable" nature [VII, 41; VIII, 65; XI, 234] are noted by Thomas Kranidas, *The Fierce Equation* (The Hague, 1965), p. 144.

17. The emphasis on "loss of society" yet mutual support is noted by Williamson, "The Education of Adam," *Milton and Others*, p. 65. Marriage as "conversation" is the argument of the Divorce Tracts. Milton defines the end of marriage again as the "pleasures of society" in "The Christian Doctrine," *Student's Milton*, p. 996.

18. Brower, *Alexander Pope*, p. 361.

PART TWO
I. Samson's "Fort of Silence"

1. For information concerning Greek tragedy and Renaissance drama available to Milton see especially: Joseph Kennard, *The Italian Theatre* (New York, 1932); Martin Mueller, "*Pathos* and *Katharsis* in *Samson Agonistes*," *ELH*, XXXI (June 1964), 156-174; W. R. Parker, *Milton's Debt to Greek Tragedy in Samson Agonistes* (Hamden, Conn., 1963).

2. Critical debate about this puzzling quality of the poem begins with Dr. Johnson, "The Rambler," No. 139, *The Works of Samuel*

Johnson, L.L.D., V (London, 1806), 399: The poem "has a beginning and an end which Aristotle himself could not have disapproved; but it must be allowed to want a middle, since nothing passes between the first act and the last, that either hastens or delays the death of Samson. The whole drama, if its superfluities were cut off, would scarcely fill a single act; yet this is the tragedy which ignorance has admired, and bigotry applauded." For a survey of recent contributions to the controversy over the structure and meaning of the poem see G. A. Wilkes, "The Interpretation of *Samson Agonistes,*" *HLQ,* XXVI (August 1963), 363-379.

3. There may also have been some theoretical reasons for the choice of this form. Perhaps Milton accepted as a rule of composition Aristotle's remark in the "Poetics," *Aristotle's Theory of Poetry and Fine Art,* ed. S. H. Butcher, 4th ed. (London, 1923), p. 109: "Tragedy like Epic poetry produces its effect even without action; it reveals its power by mere reading." Or he may have preferred, like many Italian humanists, sixteenth-century French Senecans, and their English counterparts— Samuel Daniel, Fulke Greville, Thomas Watson—to write for the educated reader rather than for a mixed theatre audience. Dryden prefers reading to performance in the "Dedication of the *Spanish Friar,*" *Essays,* I, 248: "But, as 'tis my interest to please my audience, so 'tis my ambition to be read: that I am sure is the more lasting and the nobler design: for the propriety of thoughts and words, which are the hidden beauties of a play, are but confusedly judged in the vehemence of action: all things are there beheld as in a hasty motion, where the objects only glide before the eye and disappear."

4. For discussion of the relation of the poem to oratorio, a form which also appealed to the ear rather than the eye, see G. L. Finney, "Chorus in *Samson Agonistes,*" *PMLA,* LVIII (September 1943), 649-664.

5. "Œdipus," *Works,* VI, I, i, pp. 144-145. Dryden claimed to have written Acts I and III. See MacDonald, *Dryden,* p. 118. The first scene of Sophocles' *Œdipus at Colonus* makes another interesting comparison with Milton's opening lines, for Antigone there performs the same function as Dryden's Manto by describing to her blind father their surroundings and the other characters who enter the scene. A further comparison with Euripedes' *Phoenissae* (834-835) is also pointed out by M. Y. Hughes, ed., *Paradise Regained, The Minor Poems and Samson Agonistes* (Garden City, 1937), p. 542n.

6. No extant play of either Aeschylus or Sophocles begins with a soliloquy by the protagonist, and on the rare occasions when Euripedes used such an opening (*Andromache, Iphegenia in Taurus, Helen*) the speeches are short and consist largely of a summary of the legendary events preceding the opening of the play, rather than an extended private recitation of feelings.

7. In line 336 Manoa refers to the "younger feet" of the Chorus, which comes as something of a surprise (despite Milton's designation of them in the Argument as Samson's "*equals*" or contemporaries) because the inactive role of the Chorus, their sententiousness, and their resemblance to Greek Choruses suggest they are a conventional group of "Elders."

8. The echo here of **Psalm** lviii: 4-5 is noted by Hughes, ed., *Samson Agonistes*, p. 582n.

9. This effect is noticed by Arthur Barker, ''Structural and Doctrinal Pattern in Milton's Later Poems,'' *Essays in English Literature*, ed. M. Maclure and F. W. Watt (Toronto, 1964), p. 178.

10. This ''technique of putting into the mouths of characters words that almost automatically call for a metaphorical interpretation by the Christian reader'' is discussed by William Madsen, ''From Shadowy Types to Truth,'' *The Lyric and Dramatic Milton*, ed. Joseph Summers (New York, 1965), pp. 109-110.

11. Such ''unconscious prophecies'' are discussed by Joseph Summers, ''The Movements of the Drama,'' *Lyric and Dramatic Milton*, pp. 157-158.

12. For discussion of this kind of Biblical metaphor, as distinct from allegory, see Ferry, *Milton's Epic Voice*, pp. 88-115.

13. Milton's emphasis on Samson's betrayal of a secret is mentioned by Mueller, ''*Pathos* and *Katharsis* in *Samson Agonistes*,'' p. 164.

14. The ''idea of safety in deafness'' as an allusion to the legend of the Sirens is pointed out by John Steadman, ''Dalila, the Ulysses Myth, and Renaissance Allegorical Tradition,'' *MLR*, LVII (October 1962), 560.

15. This metaphor suggests a more special definition of heroism than the traditional formula—*sapientia et fortitudo*—discussed by A. B. Chambers, ''Wisdom and Fortitude in *Samson Agonistes*,'' *PMLA*, LXXVIII (September 1963), 315-320.

16. The analogues collected by Watson Kirkconnell, *That Invincible Samson* (Toronto, 1964), follow Scripture in making Samson ask God to destroy his enemies.

17. The pun is noticed by Paul Sellin, ''Milton's Epithet *Agonistes*,'' *SEL*, IV (Winter 1964), 150.

18. For analysis of the phoenix image see Roger Wilkenfeld, ''Act and Emblem: The Conclusion of *Samson Agonistes*,'' *ELH*, XXXII (June 1965), 160-168. The word ''Holocaust'' has its original meaning of ''burnt sacrifice'' but, in the context of other comparisons with natural forces, also suggests its meaning of sweeping, destructive fire.

19. This reading is in agreement with Mueller, ''*Pathos* and *Katharsis* in *Samson Agonistes*,'' p. 158.

20. For some of the more recent examples among many interpretations of the poem as more traditionally Christian or Biblical see: Ann Gossman, ''Milton's Samson as the Tragic Hero Purified by Trial,'' *JEGP*, LXI (July 1962), 528-541; William Haller, ''The Tragedy of God's Englishman,'' *Reason and the Imagination*, ed. J. A. Mazzeo (New York, 1962), pp. 201-211; Frank Kermode, ''Milton's Hero,'' *RES*, IV (October 1953), 317-330; F. M. Krouse, *Milton's Samson and the Christian Tradition* (Princeton, 1949); Burton Kurth, *Milton and Christian Heroism* (Berkeley, 1959); T. S. K. Scott-Craig, ''Concerning Milton's Samson,'' *RN*, V (Autumn 1952), 45-53; John Steadman, '' 'Faithful Champion': The Theological Basis of Milton's Hero of Faith,'' *Anglia*, LXXVII (1959), 12-28; A. S. P. Woodhouse, ''Tragic Effect in *Samson Agonistes*,'' *UTQ*, XXVIII (April 1959), 205-222.

21. *S.A.*, 223, 422, 526, 1382.

22. A role for Samson comparable to that of Lycidas as "Genius of the shore" is argued by John Huntley, "A Revaluation of the Chorus' Role in Milton's *Samson Agonistes*," *MP*, LXIV (November 1966), 144. Similarly Arnold Stein, *Heroic Knowledge* (Minneapolis, 1957), p. 202: Samson in death has "returned to the community." The very different reading given in my chapter would seem to be supported by Milton's emphasis on Samson's role and destiny as a "Nazarite," the root meaning of which is "to separate," according to Hughes, ed., *Samson Agonistes*, p. 544n.

23. The abstract diction of these lines in no ways seems to me to suggest "a faith based on demonstration clear as geometry," as is argued by J. B. Broadbent, ed., *Milton: Comus and Samson Agonistes* (London, 1961), p. 59.

24. For a definition of this kind of Wordsworthian hero see David Ferry, *The Limits of Mortality* (Middletown, Conn., 1959), pp. 80-111.

II. *"The World Well Lost"*

1. *P.L.*, V, 570-573; VI, 298-301; VII, 112-114; VIII, 172-178.

2. This effort is described as the practice of a "theory of *neutral space*" by R. J. Kaufmann, "On the Poetics of Terminal Tragedy," *Dryden: A Collection of Critical Essays*, ed. Bernard Schilling (Englewood Cliffs, 1963), p. 90.

3. *S.A.*, 402-411; 532-540.

4. See for example "The Life of Marcus Antonius," *Shakespeare's Plutarch*, ed. T. J. B. Spencer (London, 1964), p. 199: "Antonius being thus inclined, the last and extremest mischief of all other (to wit, the love of Cleopatra) lighted on him, who did waken and stir up many vices yet hidden in him, and were never seen to any; and, if any spark of goodness or hope of rising were left him, Cleopatra quenched it straight and made it worse than before." Dryden says in the Preface to the play, *Essays*, I, 191-192: he was drawn to the story by the "excellency of the moral: for the chief persons represented were famous patterns of unlawful love; and their end accordingly was unfortunate . . . That which is wanting to work up the pity to a greater height, was not afforded me by the story; for the crimes of love, which they both committed, were not occasioned by any necessity, or fatal ignorance, but were wholly voluntary; since our passions are, or ought to be, within our power."

5. *Antony and Cleopatra*, V, ii, 82-83.

6. The deception is suggested by Charmion in *Antony and Cleopatra*, IV, xiii, 3-4, but this merely shows how well she has learned Cleopatra's ways, rather than making Cleopatra seem the tool of another's will.

7. The sea-green Syrens taught her voice their flattery;
   And, while she speaks, night steals upon the day,
   Unmarked of those that hear . . . (IV, i, p. 404)
See also II, i, p. 373: "O Syren! Syren!" Like Dalila's, Cleopatra's weapons are verbal, a suggestion which may have come to Dryden from Plutarch, "Life of Marcus Antonius," p. 203: "And, besides her beauty, the good grace she had to talk and discourse, her courteous nature that tempered her words and deeds, was a spur that pricked to the quick. Furthermore, besides all these, her voice and words were marvellous pleasant;

for her tongue was an instrument of music to divers sports and pastimes, the which she easily turned to any language that pleased her.''

8. The formula for describing his entrance sounds like similar introductions by the Chorus of other characters who visit Samson.

9. Dryden apparently recognized the special importance of this scene, since he called attention to it in the final sentence of the play's Preface, *Essays*, I, 201: ''. . . I prefer the scene betwixt Antony and Ventidius in the first act, to anything which I have written in this kind.''

10. Dryden used something like this theatrical device earlier in ''The Conquest of Granada, Part II,'' *Works*, IV, II, iv, p. 179. It may have been suggested to him by the appeals made to Shakespeare's hero by mother, wife, child and friend in *Coriolanus*, V, iii.

11. The ''externalizing of Antony's emotional commitments'' is discussed by Kaufmann, ''Poetics of Terminal Tragedy,'' p. 92.

12. Ventidius' speech combines echoes of Samson's images of suffering as the attack of insects (*S.A.*, 19-22, 623-627) with the Chorus' offer of words as ''Salve'' or ''Balm to fester'd wounds'' (*S.A.*, 184-186).

13. See for example *Antony and Cleopatra*, I, iii, 75-85. Related images for Antony's lack of an essential identity are those of the clouds (IV, xiv, 2-14) and the shadow (IV, ii, 27), which may have suggested to Dryden Antony's fantasy of blending into a landscape and Ventidius' ''Lie there, thou shadow of an emperor'' (I, i, p. 351).

14. Samson as an actor playing a role is discussed by Sellin, ''Milton's Epithet *Agonistes*,'' p. 156.

15. *All for Love*, II, i, p. 375; V, i, p. 429. A particularly telling illustration is Dolabella's appeal to Antony in III, i, p. 386: ''If you confess a man . . .'' The phrasing again suggests, not *being* a man, but claiming to be one and speaking in the style appropriate to that role. Obsession with words, names, titles, and imagery of acting parts pervades *Aureng-Zebe, Works*, V (for example I, i, pp. 213, 219, 221, 224; III, i, p. 239; V, i, p. 279), but there the device mainly expresses the arbitrary use of words as amoral instruments of the will.

16. The original suggestion comes again perhaps from Plutarch, ''Life of Marcus Antonius,'' p. 241, but it is there only an isolated observation rather than, as in *All for Love*, a characteristic formula related to other expressive devices.

17. Dryden makes much of this suggestion from ''Life of Marcus Antonius,'' especially pp. 260, 263.

18. ''Life of Marcus Antonius,'' p. 208: ''Then began Antonius with much ado a little to rouse himself, as if he had been wakened out of a deep sleep and, as a man may say, coming out of a great drunkenness.''

19. ''Life of Marcus Antonius,'' p. 267.

20. Antony's plea that Ventidius ''speak some good of me'' (V, i, p. 428) is a similar convention (taken probably from *Hamlet*, V, ii, 350-370) also contradicting what the play as a whole expresses. More suited to Dryden's meaning are Hamlet's last words: '' . . . the rest is silence'' (V, ii, 369).

21. For a discussion of this conventional formula see Reuben Brower, ''Introduction,'' *The Tragedy of Coriolanus* (New York, 1966).

INDEX